# Prais

## Tackling Bullying

'No child deserves to be bullied. This book gives teachers the tools they need to prevent pupils suffering the torment of bullying. I know what it is like to be bullied and wish this book had been there for me when I was a kid. I hope every school will have a copy.'
**Gok Wan, fashion consultant, author and television presenter**

'This is a strong book which is very accessible and it is written in a user friendly style making it suitable for the 21st century learner. It is a super resource which will be useful for trainees, CPD leaders and anyone interested in issues surrounding bullying. It includes a range of thought provoking scenarios, examples and case studies, as well as useful reading lists, top tips activities and tasks which encourage reflection.'
**Lesley-Anne Pearson, Secondary ITE Course Director, University of Huddersfield**

'A fantastic book that includes a wide range of information and practical resources that help to deal with the many aspects of the difficult topic of bullying. A must read for all teachers.'
**Samantha Goodyear, classroom teacher**

'Michele Elliott was one of the earliest people to recognise the devastating consequences of bullying and, through setting up Kidscape, to take action to tackle it. She has a wealth of experience that she shares through this book. While Elliott recognises that there is no single *magic* approach to dealing with bullying, *The Essential Guide* will empower and support all those working in schools.'
**Christopher Cloke, NSPCC**

'A book destined to be a classic – a book for using, sharing and adapting for one's own situation. Michele Elliott can be relied upon for explaining difficult behaviours and finding positive and practical solutions. All people working with children will benefit from having a copy close to hand.'
**Carrie Herbert, Chief Executive of Red Balloon Learner Centre Group: for the recovery of bullied children**

'As someone who has interviewed Michele and watched her in action I can say that she is an inspiration. Her down to earth and practical approach to tackling and managing bullying has changed the lives of many. Bullying can no longer be thought of as 'part of growing up' or something that only happens in other schools. It shouldn't be tolerated and as this book shows, it doesn't have to be. This is an invaluable and practical guide that will equip educators to tackle what can otherwise be a fraught and damaging situation.'
**Vanessa Howard, journalist and author**

# The Essential Guide to Tackling Bullying

## Other titles in the series

# The Essential Guide to Tackling Bullying

Michele Elliott

**Longman**
is an imprint of

Harlow, England • London • New York • Boston • San Francisco • Toronto • Sydney • Singapore • Hong Kong
Tokyo • Seoul • Taipei • New Delhi • Cape Town • Madrid • Mexico City • Amsterdam • Munich • Paris • Milan

PEARSON EDUCATION LIMITED

Edinburgh Gate
Harlow CM20 2JE
United Kingdom
Tel: +44 (0)1279 623623
Fax: +44 (0)1279 431059
Website: www.pearsoned.co.uk

**First published in Great Britain in 2011**

© Pearson Education Limited 2011

The right of Michele Elliott to be identified as author of this work has been
asserted by her in accordance with the Copyright, Designs and Patents Act 1988.

Pearson Education is not responsible for the content of third party internet sites.

ISBN: 978-1-4082-6483-6

*British Library Cataloguing-in-Publication Data*
A CIP catalogue record for this book can be obtained from the British Library

*Library of Congress Cataloging-in-Publication Data*
A CIP catalog record for this book can be obtained from the Library of Congress

10 9 8 7 6 5 4 3 2 1
14 13 12 11

Set in Frutiger LT Std 45 Light 10/12pt by 3
Printed in Great Britain by Ashford Colour Press Ltd, Gosport, Hampshire

# Contents

# About the author

Michele Elliott is the founder of Kidscape, the first charity in the UK set up to prevent bullying. She is a teacher, psychologist and author of over 25 books (translated into 16 languages) on parenting, bullying and child abuse. She is considered to be the leading expert on the prevention of bullying in the UK and has lectured internationally.

Michele Elliott has chaired World Health Organization and Home Office Working Groups, is a Winston Churchill Fellow, and was chosen by the charity Children and Young People Now as the 2009 Children's Champion. She was recently awarded an OBE for her work. She is on the boards of several organisations and appears frequently in the media discussing issues about children and families. Email: michele@kidscape.org.uk

# About the contributors

Linda Frost was a primary teacher and headteacher in an inner-city school for over 25 years. She has also been the manager of Kidscape's anti-bullying course, ZAP, for 10 years. She was a member of the Home Office Standing Committee on the Prevention of Child Abuse and has lectured and contributed to magazines, journals and books on child safety and bullying. Email: linda@kidscape.org.uk

Eric Jones was head of drama productions and head of fifth year at Trinity School, Croydon, having previously been deputy head of The Archbishop Michael Ramsey School, Southwark. He has conducted INSET training and conference sessions on anti-bullying, 'living with teenagers', Christian education and other skills, and has been much involved with amateur drama productions for many years. He is co-author of the *Kidscape Bullying Workshop Manual* and has written training booklets for youth groups, on story telling, drama and worship. Email: ericjones41@hotmail.co.uk

Claude Knights is the director of the children's charity Kidscape. She was previously a teacher, child guidance counsellor, university lecturer and a training manager. She has created and managed a range of professional courses, working directly with children and adults. The courses include anti-bullying strategies, child protection, behaviour management, peer counselling and mediation skills. She has been a key note speaker, both in the UK and internationally, to numerous conferences and seminars on the subject of preventing child sexual abuse and bullying. She regularly contributes to radio, television and other news media on issues relating to children. Email: claude@kidscape.org.uk

Andrew Mellor is the director of the Anti-Bullying Network. He is a Scottish teacher with 25 years' classroom experience and was a senior teaching fellow at the University of Edinburgh until 2009. He conducted the first substantial research into bullying in Scotland in 1988–90. He writes widely on the subject and lectures to a variety of audiences throughout Europe, Canada, Australia and Indonesia on developing successful approaches to bullying based on a positive whole-school ethos. Email: andrew@antibullying.net

# Introduction

This book aims to help busy teachers, headteachers and other professionals who would like suggestions, ideas and tips to deal with bullying. It includes activities that you can use to get pupils to think about and to act to prevent bullying. You can dip in and out of the chapters that are relevant to your work and the age of your pupils, or you can read every word.

You will see that I use the terms 'bully' and 'victim' throughout the book. This does not mean that we should label children as 'bullies' or 'victims' (sometimes called 'targets'). I simply use the terms for ease of reading, and to avoid saying every time 'children who are bullying' or 'children who are bullied'.

Everything in here has been tried and tested by teachers who all have many years of experience on the frontline of education. If you have suggestions that have worked for you, please let me know so that we can share them in the next edition.

You don't have time for long introductions, so please turn the page and enjoy reading!

# Bullying overview
## *Michele Elliott*

**What this chapter will explore:**

- What is bullying?
- How widespread is bullying?
- Girls and boys – bullying differently?
- The telltale signs
- Why does it matter?
- Bullies and victims
- Bystanders
- Blame or no blame?
- ZAP

This chapter provides an overview of current thinking about bullying. Later chapters will go into more detailed strategies to use in the classroom. Since there is no one totally effective and proven magic solution to bullying, this book includes many suggestions, some controversial, used by teachers to prevent and stop bullying. The reality is that sometimes one tactic works and the next time it falls flat – it may depend upon the pupils involved, the staff and the parents. So the ideas here give you a chance to see what fits with your philosophy, your school or work situation and your experience. But first we need to explore what bullying is.

## What is bullying?

Bullying is insidious, sneaking and cowardly. It is everywhere, but most especially it is in schools. Our problem as teachers is that bullying undercuts all our efforts to help pupils learn. Another problem is sorting out what bullying is so that we can try to deal with it. Defining bullying leads to lots of debate, which can be useful if you have the time. If you don't, perhaps the following definition will help:

> Bullying is deliberately harming someone who is less powerful than you with the intention of causing pain.

Bullying can be:

- Physical – the victim is pushed in the lunch queue, hit in the playground or thumped when passing someone in the hall.
- Verbal intimidation, with threats and extortion – the victim is called a slag and there is vile graffiti about them in the toilets or demands to hand over their homework or dinner money.
- Cyberbullying – using emails, websites, mobile phones and social networks to torment victims 24/7, including telling pupils to kill themselves.
- Emotional – comments that the victim is stupid and ugly and hated by the entire class.
- Exclusion – the victim suffers silent treatment, with no one talking to or supporting them or sitting with them at lunch or walking near them.
- Racist – taunting with racist remarks, gestures and graffiti.
- Homophobic – nasty comments about being gay or lesbian.

If you want to explore more about definitions of bullying there are lots of websites like www.teachernet.gov.uk you can use.

## Why not try this?

Your pupils are probably aware of what bullying is, but they may not have related their 'book' knowledge to actual incidents. Pupils sometimes think that a comment or text or email is humorous without realising that it is actually bullying. So you can either give them a list of definitions as shown on the previous page or you can use this questionnaire to start a discussion that will help them clarify what bullying is and make them think about their role in it.

### I have seen or known about incidents of:

|  | More than once | Once | Never |
|---|---|---|---|
| Physical bullying |  |  |  |
| Verbal intimidation |  |  |  |
| Cyberbullying |  |  |  |
| Emotional bullying |  |  |  |
| Exclusion |  |  |  |
| Racist bullying |  |  |  |
| Homophobic bullying |  |  |  |

Give pupils time for discussion in small groups, using questions such as:

- In your group, what kind of bullying did pupils witness or were they aware of most often? Why do you think that was the case?
- What kind of bullying is the most hidden from other pupils?
- How often do you think pupils intervene when they see bullying?
- How would you feel if any kind of bullying was happening to you or a friend?
- What could you do if you saw someone being bullied physically, verbally, etc.?

If you find your pupils do not understand some of the individual terms and want more information, you can ask them to use the internet to find out what the terms mean or give them the definitions from the previous page. Pupils may not realise that there are many forms of bullying and that they may be engaged in them almost without realising that they are bullying.

As one boy said in a group discussion: 'I was surprised at how much bullying I had seen – I didn't even consider it bullying. It was just funny. I never did it myself but I never thought how the victim felt because we were all just having a bit of fun. But it wasn't fun for him.'

# How widespread is bullying?

There is a lot of research on the extent of bullying, which can be found on sites like www.bullying.co.uk, www.kidscape.org.uk or www.nspcc.org.uk. However, research outcomes depend on the way questions are phrased and interpreted, so it is almost impossible to come up with definitive statistics. The Office for National Statistics (www.ons.gov.uk) says that 66 per cent of Year 11 pupils have complained of being bullied and that bullying was a cause of permanent exclusion in about 27 per cent of exclusions. A study by the Department for Education and ChildLine found that 51 per cent of primary pupils reported being bullied the previous term and that 54 per cent of primary and secondary pupils thought bullying was a 'big problem' in their schools (www.childline.org.uk).

You can use the questionnaires in Chapter 13 to compare what is happening about bullying in your school with studies like these, if you find it helpful.

Or it may be more relevant to use the following exercise to reflect on what you class as bullying and what is normal everyday pupil behaviour.

---

### Reflecting on practice

Would you class the following true cases as bullying or normal give and take? What is the difference between bullying and teasing? Does bullying have to be ongoing or can it be a one-off incident? Before looking at the outcome of each case, try to think about what other information you would need and what action you would take. The problem in determining what to do is that what is presented may be bullying, but it may be just pupils learning about how to interact.

- James (12) was walking home from school when Mark set upon him. Mark hit James and ran away. James had previously bullied Mark online and Mark reported it but no action was taken against James. Was it bullying?

*Outcome*: James had been bullying Mark for two years and Mark and his family were frustrated because no one stopped it. Mark's dad had arranged boxing lessons for Mark and Mark finally snapped after being attacked by James in PE that day. James left Mark alone after that but he continued to bully other pupils until he was finally suspended.

- Steve (8) was being teased about his dimples by 8-year-old Linda. He was in tears at the back of the class. Was it bullying?

*Outcome*: Steve's mum complained about the teasing, but the teacher felt it best to give Steve some ideas about what to do when Linda teased him rather than make a big deal. Steve and Linda are now friends and Linda has

---

learned that teasing is only fun when both pupils enjoy it. We also know Linda had a crush on Steve – ah, young love.

- Sarah (13) was followed into a local park by 10 boys and girls from her school. She was pushed to the ground, kicked and punched while mobile phone photographs were taken. These were posted online. When Sarah's mother called the school, she was told it was not their responsibility as it was after hours. Was it bullying?

*Outcome*: Sarah's parents called the police when the school refused to take action. The school cooperated and the bullies were charged with assault. Sarah's parents decided not to pursue the case and they moved house, putting Sarah into a new school, where she is now doing well. They are still devastated by the fact that photos of her remain online.

- Peter (7) complained to his teacher that his classmates had not let him play ball with them at break. Was it bullying?

*Outcome*: Peter did not say what he had done to his classmates – he had pushed them out of the way and grabbed the ball before they retaliated. He was reprimanded.

- Simon (16) was targeted over two years by three boys at his boarding school. He was beaten, locked out of his room, shoved outdoors in his underwear on a freezing January night and constantly subjected to taunts about his weight and comments that he was 'gay'. Was it bullying?

*Outcome*: Although the bullies were caught and one was expelled, Simon committed suicide. If Simon was gay, he did not tell anyone before he died. This is a problem for pupils who are gay or lesbian – who do they tell about the bullying if they have not come out about their sexuality?

- Leah (10) was excluded by her former friends. All the girls refused to sit with her, turned their backs on her if she approached them and ignored her. Was it bullying?

*Outcome*: Leah was more fortunate. Her teacher saw what was happening and tackled the situation by breaking up the girls, giving them assigned seats, arranging lunchroom seating and ensuring that the main bully lost her power over the group. The teacher used her influence with the parents by asking that all birthday parties should include all the girls. Only the mother of the instigator did not cooperate, thinking her daughter was the cat's pyjamas – you can't win them all. Leah is now happy and thriving.

- Jasmin (6) cried and said she was being bullied when another child took away the toy she was playing with and would not give it back. Was it bullying?

*Outcome*: Jasmin and her friends got lessons in sharing – this was not bullying!

# Girls and boys – bullying differently?

Many surveys of bullying in the 1990s, by pioneers like Professor Dan Olweus, indicated that girls were more often exposed to such bullying as spreading rumours, exclusion, verbal abuse and harassment by other female pupils, rather than physical attacks. Boys were more likely to physically attack other male pupils rather than exclude or harass them. Olweus emphasised that these gender differences were general and that there were exceptions. In a retrospective survey in the 1990s of 1,000 adults bullied as pupils, the charity Kidscape found the same pattern. It was rare for females to report physical abuse, except for things like hair pulling, while males reported mainly physical bullying by other male pupils.

In their book *No It's Not OK*, Tani Roxborough and Kim Stephenson say that male bullies seem to be more physical, impulsive and direct. These bullies enjoy the status of fighting. Female bullies plan their attacks and work in groups. They prefer emotional means such as verbal abuse and exclusion rather than physically attacking victims. Dr Tanya Beran says that research shows that physical bullying occurs more often among boys than girls at all education levels and that boys continue this right up to university (www.education.com/reference). If you want more information on girls and bullying, have a look at Valerie Besag's book *Understanding Girls' Friendships, Fights and Feuds: A Practical Approach to Girls' Bullying.*

The problem with trying to determine if girls are more verbal and boys more physical is that reports of the kinds of bullying seem to be changing. Calls to the Kidscape helpline and to other charities in the past five years suggest that bullying by girls has become more physical and that both boys and girls will physically attack one another regardless of gender. Why? We don't really know, but it may be because:

- of the rise of bullying incidents being filmed by pupils on their mobiles – it is more exciting to see someone being beaten than being yelled at;
- there are more violent female role models in films and music now than in the past;
- girls are confusing assertiveness with aggression;
- there is no longer a cultural taboo preventing boys and girls from physically bullying anyone of any gender.

Because bullying has finally become a topic of much discussion and research, it may be that all our current information about gender difference will change. Perhaps asking the pupils will be even more enlightening than what the experts have to say.

Why not try this?

Ask your pupils to discuss the issue of male and female bullying and see if they can tell whether there is a difference between the genders. Why is that? You can do this with pupils from about age eight upwards. Because there is limited research on this issue, perhaps you would like to publish results online because currently nearly everything online points to the traditional view that boys bully physically and girls emotionally.

Also, is there a gender difference in cyberbullying? Are boys more likely to cyber-bully? Do male and female bullies equally use texting to harass other pupils? For more information on cyberbullying see Chapter 4.

# The telltale signs

Pupils may indicate by signs or behaviour that they are being bullied. Sometimes this is the only clue you will have about what is happening because of the code of silence so often maintained about bullying.

You may notice pupils:

- being frightened of walking to or from school;
- being unwilling to go to school;
- changing their route to school every day, and begging parents to drive them;
- unexpectedly doing poorly in their schoolwork;
- regularly having clothes or books or schoolwork torn or destroyed;
- being worried and fearful about texts, emails and social networking sites, and showing anxiety about computer use;
- not going into the lunchroom (because their dinner money is stolen or they are reacting to taunts of 'fatty');
- starting to stammer, cry or withdraw from contact with others;
- being uncharacteristically aggressive or being caught hitting another pupil (often the victim gets caught when they finally retaliate and the cunning bully gets away, claiming it has been the victim's fault all along);
- developing stomach and headaches due to stress;
- writing stories about, talking about or attempting suicide;
- displaying unexplained bruises, scratches and cuts;
- having their possessions go 'missing';

- beginning to steal money (to pay the bully);
- refusing to say what's wrong;
- giving improbable excuses to explain any of the above.

Bullying is a likely cause of these symptoms, though obviously not the only possibility. I suggest asking pupils directly if they are being bullied. Although they may deny it initially, you can tell them you are willing to listen when and if they wish to talk. You have thrown them a lifeline.

## TOP TIP!

*Because bullied pupils often beg their parents not to tell their teacher about the bullying if they find out, you are the most important person who can spot the signs and try to help.*

# Why does it matter?

When someone is being bullied it takes over their lives. The pupil in the classroom cannot think about what you are teaching, only what will happen at break, lunch time, after school and online when they get home. If you are being bullied, the same applies – how can you think clearly about doing your best for your pupils when you don't know where the next blow will come from? So it matters that bullying can cause anxiety, destroy confidence, undermine learning, make the victims feel worthless, and can result in suicides and attempted suicides.

It matters to the bullies as well. They are not learning – they are thinking of how to continue the torment of their victims, how not to get caught and how to use the latest technology to increase their power.

## Reflecting on practice

You may be working with people in your school who believe that bullying strengthens character and teaches pupils about the real world. They may also say that too much attention is being paid to bullying and that there is now an overreaction to the issue.

What would you say?

# Bullies and victims

## What do we know about bullies?

Kidscape was the first charity in the UK set up to prevent bullying. Kidscape surveys over 30 years have found many reasons why pupils bully. Some pupils who bully are spoilt brats – overindulged by doting parents who excuse their behaviour. This kind of bully has learned to be selfish and to intimidate others to get their own way. Other pupils who bully are victims of abuse or neglect. They have been made to feel inadequate, stupid and humiliated. They lash out from their own pain. On the other hand, I have dealt with bullies who seem to be popular with other pupils. Upon closer examination it was evident that they were 'popular' because pupils hung around them to avoid becoming a victim themselves or because they thought the bully had status.

Whatever the reasons for bullying, only a small number of pupils become chronic bullies and these are the ones who cause the most problems for other pupils and for you. Isolating the power of these chronic bullies and helping them to make better choices to become better pupils is the best way forward. The problem is that this takes time, which you may not have. So in many schools the only practical solution is to exclude the bully to protect the majority of pupils. If we could change the behaviour of bullies, it would be great for everyone in school.

Bullies need help, but often reject any that is offered. Realistic, firm guidelines and rules may help them to control their reactions and lashing-out behaviour. Also trying to help them achieve some success can make a difference.

Chapter 9 gives some background and suggestions about how pupils become bullies and how to help them.

## Victims

Many pupils are one-off victims of bullying. They just happen to be in the wrong place at the wrong time. They become victims of bullying because, unfortunately, the bully chooses them to torment. If no one stops the bully, these victims start to think that they are to blame for the bullying. The reality is that the bully needs a victim. Kidscape has found that often these pupils get along quite well in one school but are victimised continually at another. This may be because of the particular mix of pupils at the schools, but more likely it is because of the policy that one school has evolved towards bullying, while the other school takes firm action against bullying.

**TOP TIP!**

*Take care not to blame the victim for being bullied – in most cases bullies need a victim and will keep going until they find one.*

A small minority of pupils seem to be perpetual victims. They are bullied no matter where they go, and it even carries on into adult life. Several people have contacted Kidscape to say that they were bullied at school from an early age. Subsequently they had been bullied all their lives – at work, in marriage and in relationships. They have developed a victim mentality and are unable to stand up for themselves. This is not their fault and in fact they are often intelligent, sensitive and creative. They have good relationships with their parents and families but can be inclined to be intense and very serious.

**TOP TIP!**

*Humour can be a great help for pupils (and you) when dealing with stressful situations. Try helping pupils develop a sense of humour – perhaps post a joke a week in the classroom or on your website.*

**Reflecting on practice**

Some teachers feel it is best just to give as good as you get. If a child reports being bullied, the response is to 'stand up to the bully or you will continue to be bullied'.

What do you think would be the outcome of this advice to pupils? Could it work?

In Chapter 8, Andrew Mellor gives some excellent suggestions for dealing with the victims of bullying.

# Bystanders

If a pupil is bullied, peer pressure sometimes makes it difficult for the victim to rally support from other pupils. As one girl told me: 'I don't like it that Holly is bullied, but I can't do anything about it or they will turn on me, too.' This 'bystander attitude' also hurts other pupils, who feel that they can't help the victim. In several schools teachers have reported how pupils who had witnessed bullying in person or online were badly affected by what they saw. Some of them felt anger, rage and helplessness. Several had nightmares and were worried that they might be the next victims. Most felt guilty that they did not stop the bullying, but really did not know how to help the victim.

One of the most effective ways to cut down on bullying is to work with the bystanders and those who are on the periphery of bullying groups. The power that bullies have is because those around them do nothing or even encourage the bullying behaviour because it causes excitement. When we remove the bystanders and the periphery group, the bully is isolated and may then be motivated to change their behaviour. Meeting with these pupils individually and removing them from the equation is a vital first step in stopping the bullying. It may be that they are told they cannot play with, eat with or be around the bully – this depends upon your school's anti-bullying policy. In a sense you are bringing them back into your code of conduct and telling them that you want them to be a positive part of the group. You are offering them better choices than the one they've made. It is important then to praise them for good behaviour. Of course this takes valuable time, but it does pay dividends. Without this peer support, the bully may try to ensnare other pupils, so it is wise to keep an eye out. What we have found is that the bully is more willing to change their behaviour when the kudos and fun of bullying is curtailed because there is no audience or applause.

## TOP TIP!

*Encourage pupils to say what they think should be done and what the problems with bystanders might be. Bystanders are key in discouraging bullying.*

# Blame or no blame?

There are many approaches to dealing with bullying:

- zero tolerance
- ignore it and it will go away
- do not keep records and never blame the bully
- peer mentoring
- reward good behaviour and give consequences to bad behaviour.

## Zero tolerance

Most teachers say that it is better to nip bullying in the bud so that all pupils know you are running a school with zero tolerance of bullying. One council has printed the word 'bullying' with a red diagonal cross like a traffic sign, which is displayed in schools. This zero-tolerance approach appears to be quite successful when staff, pupils and parents agree. Assemblies for disscussion are held, consequences to bullying are in place and no argument is allowed. The only difficulty is making sure you have all the facts and that the bullies are not getting together to put the blame on the victims. Bullies can be crafty.

## Ignore it

It is true that you can sometimes ignore low levels of bullying and that the victims will also ignore it, thus cutting off the not very determined bully. This seems to work when the intended victims are secure and the bullies are not very effective. Lucky are those who work in such a place.

## No blame

The approach of not blaming anyone for bullying allows pupils on their own with no adult interference to sort out the bullying problem. Using this approach you:

- do not try to discover factual evidence about the bullying incident or incidents;
- invite the victim of bullying to produce a piece of writing illustrating their unhappiness;
- get a group of bullies together (sometimes with other pupils included);
- share the writing of the victim's unhappiness with the group of bullies;
- do not blame anyone and say no one is in trouble or going to be punished;
- find that the group of bullies is genuinely moved by the distress of the victim and will work together to help the victim;
- never keep a written record;
- trust that the bully group will have a positive outcome.

Kidscape has a file full of complaints from parents about the 'no blame' method – several have withdrawn their pupils from schools employing it. Why? Because the bullies have no previous good relationship with the victims and use the information they get from the victims to torment them behind the backs of well-meaning teachers.

One mother wrote:

> *My son attempted suicide after his school used a no-blame approach. He was asked to write down all his feelings about the bullying and this was handed by a teacher to the bullies, who were joined by a couple of other pupils. They were supposed to find a solution. Instead the bullies found out my son's weaknesses and how vulnerable he was to what they said and did. They then pretended to my son and the teacher that they felt bad and would now be nice and support my son, raising his hopes that the bullying would end. The bullies had a great time baiting my son while acting to the teacher as if they cared. My son was so distraught that he tried to hang himself. For him there was no point in telling again when it had only made matters worse. The school clings to this policy but my son is now out of there and very happy in his new school.*

This concern about the no-blame approach is shared by leading researchers such as Professor Dan Olweus, mentioned earlier. He says that the no-blame approach does not work and that schools should not use it.

On the other hand, this approach is one that most of us have used successfully in dealing with pupils who have previously been friends and have fallen out with each other. Not apportioning blame makes good sense in cases of normal growing-up behaviour that gets out of hand.

## Reflecting on practice

Ben, Paul, Kevin and Sahir have been friends since they started school. Now aged 8, three of the boys start excluding Kevin, who is devastated by losing his friends. He sits alone at lunch and by himself at playtime. You notice this and talk to each pupil individually to find out what has happened. There is nothing earth-shattering and you get them to talk together. Kevin tells them how sad he is and the boys say sorry and things return to normal. This is obviously better than coming down like a ton of bricks and the boys learn how their actions affect others.

## TOP TIP!

*Using any approach depends upon the maturity of your pupils and their ability to be empathetic. Victims should not feel they have been exploited to teach others empathy – it isn't fair to them.*

## Peer mentoring

Letting the pupils become involved through schemes like peer mentoring can be a wonderful solution if you have all the right support in place (see Chapter 11 for details). These schemes obviously need training, backup and supervision from teachers, but they have been enormously successful. Some schools have even installed their own anti-bullying helplines.

## Rewards and consequences

Rewarding good behaviour and giving consequences for bad behaviour may seem logical and like good parenting. But there is debate even over this simple concept. Some feel that you are making a value judgement. Well, yes you are, and why not? Being nice to people is good, bullying is bad. That doesn't mean we have to label the bully as bad, but their behaviour certainly is. Also there is a controversy about giving consequences like missing a school trip, detention or eating lunch alone. Is this punishment and should it be used in schools? More on this in Chapters 9 and 13.

### Reflecting on practice

- What do you think about using the various approaches to bullying?
- Do you support blame or no blame?
- What about using consequences?
- Are 'consequences' the same as 'punishment'?

# ZAP

Ending this chapter on a positive note, let me tell you about ZAP. Kidscape has been holding free courses for over 10 years for pupils aged 9 to 16 who have been severely bullied. They come to our one-day course called ZAP and learn ways to feel better about themselves and become more self-assertive. During the day they meet others who have experienced bullying and learn techniques and strategies that help them stop thinking of themselves as victims. One boy said that he went back to school and pretended that the bullying did not bother him and eventually the acting turned into reality. Another pupil said how good it was to meet others who had been through similar experiences and that she did not feel she was the only one any more. Many of the pupils keep in contact with one another. The parents also meet during that day and we help them to find ways to reduce the bullying and the stress on their own families.

You might ask why the victims come and why not hold courses for bullies instead. You may not be surprised to find out that the bullies and their parents do not seem to be willing to come. But Kidscape is still trying and hopes to succeed in giving help to these families. So the next best thing is to try to help the victims. The sad fact is that the bullies, if not stopped, move on to another victim, creating yet another participant for ZAP.

The good news is that, after ZAP, the bullying stops in about 70 per cent of cases, according to follow-up surveys and independent research. You can use some ZAP strategies in a less intense way in the classroom. I will be talking about some of them in Chapter 12. If you would like to know more, contact Kidscape via the website (www.kidscape.org.uk).

After one of the ZAP days, Kidscape received this letter from a mother:

> I'm writing to express my heartfelt thanks. As you know my daughter Ellie attempted suicide after years of bullying. The final straw was the Hate Eli website set up by her former friends. I talked to your helpline adviser and you invited Ellie on your ZAP course. I can only say the change has been miraculous. The terrified, crying girl who came into your office that morning was transformed by the end of the day.

> Ellie was absolutely skipping down the road when we left, after the most positive and fabulous course. Since coming to Kidscape, Ellie has begun to smile, laugh and even sing again. When one of the bullies confronted her, Ellie looked her in the eye and said, 'If you were a nicer person I might feel like being your friend.' Then she walked away! How's that for a result?

# Conclusion

Bullying will never go away completely, but by condemning bullying behaviour and acting to stop it, we can prevent thousands of pupils suffering. After all, we used to shove pupils up chimneys and stuff them down mines. Now, that would seem totally unacceptable. In the past 25 years the idea of bullying has finally become unacceptable. The good news is that now the vast majority of schools recognise that bullying is a problem and that most teachers want to see it stamped out altogether. As one teacher commented, 'It's a lot easier to teach kids who aren't tied up in knots about what's going to happen to them at break. It's good to see the former bullies (some used to frighten me) feeling better about themselves. Maybe they are finally learning a bit of maths!'

## Going further

### Useful websites

www.bullying.co.uk

www.childline.org.uk

www.education.com/reference/article/difference-between-boy-and-girl-bullies

www.kidscape.org.uk

www.nspcc.org.uk

www.ons.gov.uk

www.stonewall.org.uk

www.teachernet.gov.uk

### Books on bullying

Besag, V., *Understanding Girls' Friendships, Fights and Feuds: A Practical Approach to Girls' Bullying* (Open University Press, 2006).

Elliott, M. and Kilpatrick, J., *How to Stop Bullying, A Kidscape Training Guide* (Kidscape, 2002).

Olweus, D., *Bullying at School: What We Know and What We Can Do* (Blackwell, 1993).

Roxborough, T. and Stephenson, K., *No It's Not OK* (Penguin, 2007).

# Chapter 2

# Discouraging bullying
## *Michele Elliott*

### What this chapter will explore:

- Bullying at the school-wide level
- Bullying at the classroom level
- Bullying at the individual level

It would be lovely to set up a school from scratch that somehow stopped all bullying. It is possible, but only if you have one pupil and one teacher and they get along all the time. Whenever a group of pupils gets together, you have the potential for a bullying situation. Bullying is a fact of life, but there is much we can do to discourage it. Some schools have done amazing work and I would like to share their successful ideas.

# Bullying at the school-wide level

Bullying is more common in some schools than others. Why? Because it seems some schools deny it happens and therefore it continues. Others are too busy to deal with it or have an ethos of bullying from the head down and woe betide the teacher who tries to change things. Fortunately, more and more schools now take bullying seriously and staff do their best to eradicate it.

All schools are required to have an anti-bullying policy. If you are currently teaching, do you know what and where yours is? Is it effective? Were you involved in writing it? Some schools download an anti-bullying policy from the internet, including the one on the Kidscape website; others modify or write their own by holding meetings and involving staff, pupils and parents. No prizes for guessing which are most effective.

Ideally your anti-bullying policy should include a definition of bullying, how incidents will be recorded, what consequences there will be and how to involve parents. It should be posted on the school's website and be used when bullying situations arise. A good and well-integrated anti-bullying policy is essential. The only caveat is not to drag out the discussion to the point that nothing gets done.

## Physical space issues

In addition to the anti-bullying policy, here are just a few physical space issues you may want to take into account:

● How does the layout of the school either contribute to or discourage bullying?

● What are the arrangements for changing classes or moving groups of pupils?

● What are the trigger points that have led to problems in the past? For example, too many pupils passing through narrow corridors and doorways inviting shoving and pushing, or toilets that have long queues of hyperactive pupils.

● Where are the supervisors in the playground – with the pupils or talking in the corner?

● How is the outside space organised? Is there enough room for pupils to pursue different activities without irritating one another? (See www.kidscape.org.uk to download '20 ways to a safer playground'.)

● What about bushes, hidden corners and other places that bullying can take place without anyone seeing or hearing it?

● If school buses are used, what about the supervision at the gate and on the bus?

- If parents collect and drop off pupils, is it a free-for-all?
- Where is the staffroom in relation to the classrooms and playground?
- What happens if you have graffiti on walls or litter in the playground?
- What happens at lunch time? Is the system orderly and conducive to cooperation between pupils?

What we know is that the school itself sends an important message to pupils about how they should behave. Day after day of shoving to get to class, anxiety on the bus, waiting to grab lunch and gobble it down (sounds like a teacher's day, right?) does create a non-caring atmosphere. Some things you can do nothing about, but there may be ways to make things better. For example, in one of the schools I visited, the staff decided to get parents in to help redesign the outdoor area. In place of dead, weedy bushes, some flowers and low plants were put in at very little cost. It sounds too simple, but it made a big difference to how the pupils acted.

## Why not try this?

This is an excellent exercise that might give you ideas about possible changes and also tell you where bullying is happening.

Ask each class to design the perfect school for bullying. You might want to divide the class into smaller groups. Give each group a piece of A3 paper and tell them to draw the building, including lunchroom, PE areas, playground, corridors, classrooms, etc. Alternatively you can have them draw your own school with all of the above.

After they do that, ask them to put an X where bullying might or does happen.

This is also a good exercise for staff and, if you have people with a sense of humour within your staff, can become hilarious. A little hilarity is a good thing, given the many tensions during a normal school day.

Once you have mapped where most of the Xs are, you can see if there are ways to minimise opportunities for bullying. In one school I worked with, the real problems were when pupils passed through the corridors, so the teachers simply stood in the doorways during those times. The playground was also a problem, so the headteacher installed a camera trained on the hot spots – and lo and behold, bullying was reduced dramatically.

Peter Stephenson and David Smith, two eminent psychologists, created a 20-point list from a mythical management consultant about how to encourage bullying in school. Their suggestions included ensuring that teachers arrive late, that materials and equipment be in short supply, that there is no liaison between departments, and that records should not include details about bullying or what actions were taken in any bullying incident. You may want to make your own list. One headteacher looking at the 20 points declared it was obviously based entirely on his school, especially the late arrival of teachers.

These ideas can lead to good discussion about what could be done to change things for the better. And it is more fun than just droning on about how bad things are.

## Cyberbullying

An area that is now of paramount importance is the school's computer system. Since cyberbullying has become such a pervasive problem, ensuring that staff are trained in how to spot and deal with cyberbullying is essential. Mobile phone cameras and videos are another area of technology that has been hijacked by bullies. Some schools forbid pupils having mobiles during school hours. Chapter 4 includes advice about cyberbullying and activities for pupils. Pupils know more about this kind of bullying than most teachers and it is helpful to get not only their input on what is happening but also their ideas to combat it. In Chapter 13 there are more suggestions and sample questionnaires to find out what pupils know about bullying that is happening out of the sight of staff.

## Positive role models

Schools with the most effective anti-bullying ethos are those run by a headteacher who is not a bully and who not only believes in zero tolerance of bullying, but also leads from the front and supports staff. This person ensures that the pupils, staff and parents know that bullying will be dealt with swiftly, that there will be consequences and that everyone has a duty to tell if they know about bullying of any kind, including cyberbullying. I have run workshops for very frustrated teachers who want to change things but are up against non-supportive headteachers. But even in those cases, teachers have quietly and resourcefully worked with their own classes to ensure their pupils learn how to behave properly. This is not easy, but those teachers are making a difference. Pupils need these role models of good behaviour.

Recently I talked to a conference of teachers and asked if they would raise their hand if they could remember the name of a favourite influential teacher they had in school. Nearly everyone could. I remember my Year 9 biology teacher, Mr Soper, who gave me the confidence to pursue science and whose homilies I can still recite. Teachers do make a difference.

**Reflecting on practice**

Looking at your own school, these are the important questions:

- If the building and grounds are good for bullies to ply their trade, what effective changes could be made with the least cost?
- If nothing can be done, is it possible at least to put in more supervision at potential trouble spots?
- How can you improve your school ethos?
- Are there parents who would make it a project to improve the playground?
- What other ideas do you have?

**TOP TIP!**

*Online systems to monitor and record behaviour, including bullying incidents, can be a real help. You can find out about them from websites like www.schoolbehaviour.co.uk and www.teachers2parents.co.uk (note, however, that these services are not free unless your local authority is providing them).*

# Bullying at the classroom level

The classroom, your home from home, can affect how your pupils interact.

My first classroom was painted dull grey, had dirty windows and very little ventilation. My 36 Year 6 pupils and I tried our best to liven it up, but it was hard going. With so many pupils and that environment, it was a constant struggle to keep the pupils who were disruptive from picking on others. That classroom and the size of the class contributed to a bullying ethos. I was constantly fighting fires and certainly learned a lot. Studies show that class size can affect how successful you are in combating bullying, but that is just plain common sense. The fewer pupils you have, the easier it is to keep an eye on them and to prevent bullying.

No doubt you are thinking, 'I have no choice about the classroom I am assigned to and the number of pupils put in my class.' True. But are there some things you can do to make life easier for you and your pupils?

## Why not try this?

If, like many teachers, you work in an old building, chances are that your classroom needs help. One newly qualified teacher spent a weekend painting his classroom, although he then got in trouble for 'health and safety' because he used a ladder and did not get advance permission. In a school with good parental support, you may be able to arrange help to improve classrooms. In the inner-city Victorian school where I was a governor, we managed to get parents to revamp the playground, which made a huge difference to the behaviour of the pupils.

You are probably already adept at using pupils' work or posters to try to make the classroom a pleasant place for you and your class. I have been in some classrooms that I would happily move into and others where it is clear that the teacher thinks it is enough just to exist. The difficulty for teachers is the number of tasks they face every day, so that the classroom environment can be neglected. In one pupil survey of 13-year-olds about what they thought about their school, several classroom issues stood out:

- boring lessons
- teachers who dressed the same every day
- other pupils in class who were 'stupid', 'weird' or 'irritating'
- peeling paint on the walls (which the pupils helped along)
- never-changing wall posters (in one history class, the posters depicting the War of the Roses were still there months later when the class was studying the World Wars).

## TOP TIP!

Bring some plants into your classroom and get the pupils to help take care of them. Or bring cut flowers, and when they start to fade, comment that it would be nice to have replacements – shameless, I know, but you may get a flower supply all year round!

These ideas may seem inconsequential and not related to bullying, but we know from talking to bullies that many problems happen when these pupils are not engaged. Changing the classroom environment and surprising pupils with new things to look at – even if they don't pay attention to your stimulating lessons – is one small thing teachers can do.

Like the pupils, the teachers had their own list of complaints, but I am sure you are familiar with those from your own experiences.

## Why not try this?

Depending upon the age of the pupils you teach, you can encourage positive common activities with the pupils in your classroom. The comments about other pupils being strange or weird mean that bullies feel it is OK to torment them. Instead, try some anti-bullying classroom activities to build empathy:

- Implement a classroom anti-bullying code by asking the pupils to come up with a simple code that everyone follows while in your class.

- Have a contest to come up with simple slogans, which are then made into posters and are displayed or even printed on T-shirts. Give a prize for the most popular slogans — something inexpensive or maybe extra time at a favourite activity.

- Try an idea from Norway, where all the classrooms I visited from ages 7 to 16 had photos of the pupils with positive remarks on paper just below the photos. The remarks were made by other pupils and by teachers.

- Give a prize once a week or month to a pupil who has done something kind. For younger pupils, tried and tested star charts are still effective and popular for encouraging good behaviour.

- Try giving out five stars at the beginning of each week to each pupil. If they all behave and do not bully anyone, they keep their stars and the entire class gets a treat on Friday. But if a pupil bullies another pupil, stars are removed for each incident and can only be reinstated by apologies and acts of kindness. You can also use this technique in a different way by working up from no stars to five. The peer pressure to be nice is overwhelming!

- Use class meeting techniques such as the 'talking stick' or 'circle time'. These techniques have been used successfully for decades — certainly when I was doing teacher training in the 1960s. The idea is to hold a weekly meeting that allows pupils to bring up ideas and concerns, and show support for one another. The talking stick comes from Native American tribes, where one person in the circle is given the stick and allowed to talk while others listen with respect. Similarly, in circle time an object, like a ball or stuffed toy, is held by the speaker, who passes it on to others. No one has to talk, but you have the right to talk when you hold the object. There has to be a limit on time and ground rules for listening, and you may want to choose a topic like cyberbullying.

The reality is that we cannot control how pupils are brought up and their home environment, but we can give them a measure of stability in class and a possibly different outlook on how to behave. It is worth a try (see Chapters 12 and 13 for more ideas).

## Bullying at the individual level

When you suspect that bullying is going on, it is important to find out as quickly as possible what is happening. The longer bullying is allowed to fester, the more difficult it is to sort out. By talking to both the victims and bullies, you may be able to stop the bullying before it gets completely out of hand. The main problem is protecting the victims and finding out the truth – or as much of the truth as you can. You can only do this if the school anti-bullying policy is operating effectively. If the policy states that bullying will not be tolerated and that everyone is expected to tell if they know anything about any bullying that is happening, pupils will be more inclined to tell. The message for the victim has to be 'Your safety and well-being is important' and so by telling then things should improve and will not get worse. Bystanders must know they will get into trouble if they do not intervene, tell or get help if they know someone is being bullied. The message for bullies is that the bullying will stop and stop immediately.

When you talk to pupils who say they are being bullied, you quickly realise how anxious they are about telling. The code of pupils about not 'grassing' to adults is strong, and victims are usually threatened by the bullies that things will 'get worse' if they tell. Many pupils think that it is better to suffer and hope that things will improve. This gives the bully even more power and is actually harmful for both the bully and victim: the victim continues to be tormented, while the bully feels invincible and learns that bullying pays (see Chapter 9).

### Why not try this?

If your school does not have and cannot afford the kind of online monitoring service mentioned earlier, then another way to get information about bullying is the physical 'suggestion box'. You can also use email or texts to communicate in confidence with pupils. The idea is that anyone can put a suggestion about homework, lunches, the playground, etc., or about a bullying situation into the box attached to the wall or through a system set up via computer that is secure. This works when the school has a clear anti-bullying ethos. Bystanders, friends or the victim can put a note saying that bullying is happening out of sight of the teachers at a certain time and place. Teachers can then look out for it and catch the bullying in the act, which means the victim does not have to tell. The only problems are time and that the bullies could set up a situation in which it seems the victim is at fault. No method is foolproof, but this has worked well for some teachers.

## Finding out

Parents should let you know if their child is being bullied, but victims will often plead with their parents not to talk to the teachers. I have held meetings with parents who are trying to tell me that their child is a victim of bullying but they cannot seem to say it directly. This does not help anyone – victims or bullies. If parents know and you do not know, the bullying will probably continue. Silence is the best friend of the bully. After some frustrating discussion I got to the point of just asking parents directly if their child was being bullied and telling them that I would do my best to uncover the bullying myself. That way it appeared to the child that I was the bright spark who found out.

We all know that bullying is often not clear cut and that sometimes both parties are to blame. However, bullies can be excellent manipulators and can muddy the waters – much to the distress of victims and their families, who often feel that justice is not done.

It does help to give parents a letter or email explaining the school's policy on bullying (see Chapter 13). Make sure parents realise that you want to know if they find out that their child or any other pupil is being bullied.

> **TOP TIP!**
>
> *Even if you put your anti-bullying policy on your website, a personal letter or email to parents at the beginning of the school year means that everyone knows the rules. It will save you time discussing such things as 'No one ever told me that'.*

## Tackling bullying at the individual level

My colleagues and teachers I have met on workshops have given me great suggestions about dealing with bullying at the individual level:

- Talk in private to the possible victim at a time when other pupils are not aware of it happening. In one school the headteacher hands out passes to pupils once a month and that gives each pupil a time alone when they can safely tell if they or anyone they know is being bullied.

- If necessary, be in contact with the parents of the victim to work out ways to deal with the problem (see Chapter 10).

- Assure the victim that they will be protected and that it is right that you know what is happening.

- Be aware that bullies are clever and skilful at diverting attention from themselves, blaming others and talking their way out of trouble. They say things like the victim started it, it was only teasing, it was an accident or you are always picking on them.

- Remove the bully from the situation and explain why they are being excluded.
- If there is a serious assault, contact the police.
- There usually is a group of bullies who all support the main bully. If this is the case, never talk to them together. Ask each person alone what happened and how they are going to fix it. Then bring them together and have them repeat what they said to you in private so they cannot pretend to one another that they pulled the wool over your eyes. The power of the group needs to be broken so that the person or maybe two who are leading it no longer have an audience and support group. This was one of the main suggestions from a group of young offenders who had been convicted of crimes that ranged from stealing to assault. When I questioned them about how they behaved at school, it was no surprise to find out that over 90 per cent had been part of a bully gang. As Jack, the bully in *Lord of the Flies* (by William Golding), said: 'Who will join my tribe and have fun?'
- Do not accept excuses for bullying – make it clear that in your school there are no excuses for any kind of bullying.
- Change classroom seats, breaks, lunchroom times and classes, and stagger leaving times if this helps eliminate bullying.
- Draw up contracts of behaviour that are signed by pupils and are known about by parents.

Older, responsible pupils can be instrumental in helping with the problem of bullying. They can:

- be a point of contact for frightened younger pupils, rather like older brothers and sisters;
- act as monitors;
- use drama and role-play activities about bullying;
- run assemblies.

You probably have 20 more ideas. Let me know for the next edition.

## Reflecting on practice

It is useful to have a fledgling idea about what you can do about bullying and potential bullying with your pupils. It is not always possible to decide in advance what will happen, but it is possible – and useful – to think about what you might do in some cases. Most of the cases below are applicable to both primary and secondary schools.

- Your anti-bullying policy is sitting somewhere in a filing cabinet or on a shelf. It has not been looked at for three years and no one seems to care or be worried about it. You are a new teacher to this school and in your previous school you had an excellent, well-thought-out policy.

  *What could you do?*

- You have a problem with four girls in your class who always sit together and make comments and refuse to let any other pupils join them. They are annoying you and the other pupils.

  *What could you do?*

- Your pupils will not allow one boy to play games with them in the playground. He seems to be shy and hangs around the edge of the games. In class he is having trouble with learning basic skills like reading and is behind most of the other pupils.

  *How can you help him?*

- You know that the main area where pupils are bullied by older pupils is the toilets.

  *Any ideas?*

- You are approached after school by a boy who wants to talk to you in confidence. He asks you to promise not to do anything if he tells you about a friend who is being bullied online and being attacked on the way home from school. The bullying is not taking place on school grounds and the cyberbullying is being conducted from a home computer.

  *What do you say to him?*

- You find out that three girls from your school are following home a younger girl (also one of your pupils) and making cruel comments, pushing her, pulling her hair and taking her money. They are also taking photos of their abuse with their mobiles and putting them online. The victim has not said anything but does seem withdrawn lately. You know the identity of the victim but not the bullies.

  *What do you do?*

- A boy in your class is hanging out after school with an older group of boys. You know these boys have been bullying pupils, but they have never been caught. They have been accused but the victims always recant out of fear. Your pupil's behaviour has changed and he is becoming a bit of a bully during break time.

  *What do you do about your pupil?*

- You suspect that a girl in your class is being bullied. She is showing many of the signs mentioned in Chapter 1.

Her schoolwork is starting to go downhill and she is not eating lunch. You notice that her weight seems to be dropping and her energy levels are low.

*What would you do?*

These are just a few possible cases. You will probably have many more and some that might be much more serious. For example:

● You have been told by a pupil that another pupil is threatening to commit suicide because of bullying. You talk to the pupil who is supposed to be suicidal and he says he was only joking. However, you have a gut feeling that he is in danger.

*Do you contact another teacher, headteacher or his parents? If you do, are you making matters worse? If you don't, and he does attempt suicide or even succeed, where does that leave you?*

The fact that every year several pupils commit suicide because of bullying is extremely distressing, but it has become a fact of life and needs to be thought about and discussed. Fortunately it is still rare and let's hope it stays that way.

## Conclusion

We have to keep in mind that most pupils get through school without major bullying and that it is the few chronic bullies who create most of the problems. But the problems they create can destroy the good work done by you, as you try your best to set up a safe, healthy place for pupils to learn. There are some things that can be done with the school and classrooms, but the main work is with the individuals. Having a firm anti-bullying policy, support from the headteacher and consequences that are known by all will help to discourage bullying. It may take an extra effort at the beginning of the school year to put up as many obstacles to bullying as possible, but it does make the rest of the year easier for everyone.

## Going further

**Useful websites**

www.kidscape.org.uk

www.schoolbehaviour.co.uk

www.teachers2parents.co.uk

**Research on bullying**

Stephenson, P. and Smith, D., 'Why some schools don't have bullies', in M. Elliott, *Bullying: A Practical Guide to Coping for Schools* (Pearson, 2002).

# Teachers are key
## *Michele Elliott*

**What this chapter will explore:**

- Preventing bullying
- The importance of self-esteem
- Pupil–teacher relationships
- Allowing bullying
- Encouraging bullying
- The power of the positive

In Chapter 2 we talked about how individuals are vital in discouraging bullying. The key individuals in the school are the teachers. You are the arbitrator, the role model, the one who pupils look to as a safety net if they are being bullied. Even if you are in a school that needs to improve its record on preventing bullying, when you are in your classroom and with your pupils you can still make a difference.

# Preventing bullying

Several years ago a man named Frank sent me this letter:

> It began on my first day of school. The teacher left the room for a brief moment and I was instantly surrounded by a mob of kids all laughing and shouting at me. I was born with crossed eyes and was small for my age. 'Freak, look at his eyes, ugly' were just a few of the things they said. I was so terrified that I broke a pencil I held in my hand. The teacher returned and found me in the middle of the unruly group and blamed me for the chaos. From then on I was the object of continual bullying. I know it's a hell of a responsibility being a teacher, but I can't help thinking how different it would have been if she had taken the time to find out the real story. Still, she is forgiven now.

> It seemed the whole mob chased me and tormented me constantly. I was alone and became what I now know was withdrawn and virtually paranoid. What really hurt was not knowing why they did it. I was always so nice to everyone. I couldn't figure out why the teachers didn't stop it. They must have known.

> The early attacks were because I looked funny to other children. The later ones happened because I was withdrawn and seemed strange. The other children were so awful to me that I did not want anything to do with them and tried to keep myself to myself for my own protection. So I was in a no-win situation.

> When I read about bullying it sets off my bad memories and I am overwhelmed with anger, rage and tears, as though it was happening all over again, even 45 years later.

> Please tell teachers never to tell a child to take no notice. If a child complains about bullying, he or she must be desperate and only adult intervention will help.

> I hope my story may help to stop this happening to other children. I am able to write to you calmly now because I am undergoing therapy and coming to terms with the nightmare that was my school days.

If you were facing your pupils in the first week of school and wanted to ensure that you had done everything possible to prevent bullying in your classroom, what do you need to know?

# The importance of self-esteem

Research by Christina Salmivalli found that pupils with high levels of self-esteem had the confidence to go to the aid of victims when they witnessed bullying. She also found that pupils who reported being bullied had lower self-esteem than those who were not bullied. Of course that could be because the bullying itself destroyed the self-esteem of the victims. Whatever the reason, the implication is that if you work on the self-esteem of your pupils, you may be able to reduce bullying.

## TOP TIP!

*Remember the words of Eleanor Roosevelt, one of the most influential women of her time and a champion of human rights, who said: 'Nobody can make you feel inferior without your permission.'*

## Why not try this?

Ask your pupils to work in small groups and come up with a definition of self-esteem. This can be brief and may include things such as:

- liking yourself
- feeling good about what you do
- valuing yourself
- believing in yourself.

Then ask them to compile a list of 10 ways people can protect, improve or reinforce self-esteem. One group came up with:

1 Pat yourself on the back for your successes.

2 Stay away from nasty people who put you down.

3 Do not believe negative things said by others about you.

4 Develop your talents and interests.

5 Do things that make you feel good and that you are good at.

6 Spend time with people who like you.

7 Always do what you think is right.

8 Treat others with respect.

9 Set goals and work hard.

10 Make your own choices and don't allow others to lead you.

With younger pupils you can explain self-esteem with the simple words above, such as liking yourself, and ask them to think of three things they like about themselves. If you have pupils who cannot think of any ways they like themselves, have a few ideas you can give them. For example:

- You are a good friend.
- You work hard in art, maths, reading or another subject.
- You are liked by others.

**TOP TIP!**

*Teachers with high self-esteem also produce pupils with high self-esteem – no surprise there. So feeling good about yourself will pay dividends when working with pupils. Think of some things you like about yourself.*

**Why not try this?**

A brief and easy lesson that you can use is to get each pupil to say or write down one positive thing about each member of the class. Writing is best if you are worried that some pupils might not be nice; you can monitor the comments if necessary. At the end of the ZAP session mentioned in Chapter 1, pupils of all ages are given a piece of paper, which is attached to their back. Every participant goes around and writes something positive on every other participant's paper. You should see the joy on the faces of the pupils as they read the comments. It really boosts their self-esteem. Parents have later said that their children keep the papers and reread them.

A variation on this idea is to ask pupils to write down five positive things about themselves. If they have difficulty doing this, suggest they include talents or aspirations for the future, like becoming a poet or racing-car driver. The object is to get them to stop focusing on what they perceive as negative about themselves.

You can also ask pupils to write down 10 words that describe themselves. They can then arrange these in order of what they like most about themselves and what they like least. You can help them add strengths that you see in them but they might not realise they have.

# Pupil–teacher relationships

When pupils feel they are respected and they respect you as someone who does not bully or misuse your power, they will be less likely to bully in your classroom. They will also be more likely to tell you about bullying because they trust you. And the earlier you know about bullying incidents, the easier it is to stop them.

Why not try this?

## Why not try this?

You could have a time each week when your pupils meet to talk and share. In Norway, where I visited many schools, all pupils at every level had a weekly meeting. They sat in a circle with a teacher and every pupil could talk if they wished. The ground rules were simple: you could bring up any issue like bullying or your dog's latest trick or a concern you had about homework, but you had limited time. One especially bright young teacher used this time to ask her pupils to rate if they felt happy or sad that day on a scale of 1 to 10. She individually followed up any pupil who rated themselves 5 or below. Time consuming, but what a great way to keep in tune with her pupils.

## Make time for pupils to talk to you privately

It is asking a lot, but if you establish private time with each pupil in advance of any bullying problems, you will be able quietly and effectively to find out what is happening and protect pupils from being labelled a 'grass'. You may have informed all pupils that your school is a telling school and everyone is expected to tell about bullying, but some pupils will still try to make others stay silent by claiming they are grassing.

If you do find out about bullying, you can then uncover it yourself, protecting your 'source'. For example, if you hear that there is bullying going on in the toilets at a certain time, you can just happen to be there and see it for yourself. That way the victim cannot be harassed for telling.

## Classroom seating

In Chapter 2 changing pupils' seating arrangements was mentioned. If you notice that certain groups of pupils only sit with each other, change your seating plan before bullying develops. You can tell if pupils are beginning to become exclusive to the detriment of the class as a whole. How about establishing right from the start that you are going to assign seats and change them frequently? That could avoid future difficulties, and mixing up the pupils also keeps them alert.

# Allowing bullying

You may have worked with teachers who have the attitude that they are there to teach, not to babysit or sort out the behaviour of pupils. Some of these teachers, by their actions, attitude and lack of intervention, are giving a clear message to the bullies that they won't be interfered with. Teachers and other members of staff who do that are allowing bullying to thrive.

How do you *allow* bullying to go on? In my first school there was a teacher who taught me how to allow bullying and bad behaviour to flourish. His classroom had no decoration and his lessons were dull, but his true talent was his complete lack of discipline and caring. He had no respect for his pupils except his favourites. His favourites were the bullies. He liked their 'spunk'. In the staffroom he would go on and on about the 'weak, lily-livered, milk-toast' pupils who did not know how to stand up for themselves. 'Little cry babies,' he would say with contempt. He praised those who did not take any 'cr**', and he always seemed to have time to spend with them. He would say he did not encourage bullying, but he gave strong signals that he did not have time to listen to tales of woe from victims of bullying.

He let pupils know that power was all important and that he respected those who wheedled power. To ask for help or admit to being bullied was a sign of weakness. The pupils who hung around him were bright enough but became very full of themselves and their own power, which they used to pick on others. With the right teacher, these pupils would have used their admittedly outgoing personalities in a more positive way.

So, you allow bullying by:

- ignoring it;
- denying it;
- allowing pupils to get away with bullying;
- giving pupils too much power without limits.

This teacher finally retired, much to the relief of most, but the legacy he left those pupils was they were better off if they were not empathetic and they just took what they wanted. They used the power he allowed them to have to make life miserable for those the teacher did not like or respect. In his world, that included the 'nerdy', intellectual, musical, creative, sensitive pupils – the kind that grow up to contribute to society. Thank goodness there are not many teachers like him ... or are there?

Although you probably cannot change the ways of teachers who allow bullying to go on, perhaps they will hear about your lessons in self-esteem and wake up. Or maybe you can do the following exercise with your pupils and put the results in the staffroom.

There is a children's song called 'There's a hole in my bucket'. Henry sings to Liza about the hole and she tells him to fix it. He asks with what should he fix it. It goes on and on and is quite fun. You can find the lyrics on the internet.

Make a leap and think of a person being a bucket full of self-esteem. The hole in the bucket is caused by the self-doubt brought on as negative comments, thoughts and actions of others, which puncture the bucket. Ask your pupils to come up with a list of the things that people do to themselves or others that poke holes in the bucket of self-esteem.

Let other staff know you are doing this exercise and, who knows, it just might prick the conscience of that negative teacher. Anyway, it is a good exercise for your pupils.

# Encouraging bullying

And then there are the teachers who go that little bit further than allowing bullying – they actually encourage bullying, and may even bully the pupils themselves. In fact these are teachers who should get out of teaching – many are bitter and disillusioned, and take it out on everyone around them. In my experience it is not the new, enthusiastic teachers who encourage bullying. Nor is it most of the teachers with long service, who feel that teaching is a profession. It is the teachers who are only teaching because it brings in a salary and do not enjoy what they are doing who are the ones who seem to encourage bullying. Many are bullies themselves.

How do teachers *encourage* bullying? A young man I met told me this story:

*When I was 14 one of my teachers – for some reason I still cannot figure out – took a dislike to me. I was a good kid, never in trouble, had friends and did well in other classes, and other teachers seemed to like me. Perhaps I was quiet and maybe a bit sensitive. I don't know. Anyway, this teacher made it his mission to say bad things about my work in front of other pupils. He rolled his eyes if I asked a question and ignored me if I had my hand up to answer a question or contribute to the class. This made me desperate to get him to like me and I redoubled my efforts. I always got my assignments in on time and worked extra hard in his class. It didn't matter and only seemed to irritate him.*

*One day he gave me a really low mark, the lowest in the class, on something I had worked hard to do. I plucked up the courage to talk to him after school and went into his classroom. He was working at his desk and glanced up. When he saw me, he looked back down and continued to work, refusing even to acknowledge that I was in the room. I stood there awkwardly for what seemed an eternity and finally turned around and fled. The rest of the year I shut down in his class, continued to get low marks and never told my parents because I was ashamed and knew it must be my fault.*

*One of the offshoots of this teacher's behaviour to me was that a couple of pupils in the class got the message that it was OK to bully me whenever we were in that class or near that teacher. These were pupils the teacher liked and praised. The bullies made my life hell and knew that they had the backing of the teacher.*

*Years later I met other pupils who said they remembered this teacher and that he always had pupils he picked on in each class and no one dared to remonstrate with him. Now I realise that he was a crusty, old, negative guy who should have dug ditches instead of teaching, but it took me years to get over his abuse.*

Teachers encourage bullying by:

- selecting pupils on whom they offload their own hang-ups;
- ensuring that they pick on these pupils in front of other pupils;
- sending a message to the victims that they are worthless and inadequate;
- creating a hostile climate that lets bullies thrive;
- targeting pupils who they perceive as vulnerable and maybe different in some way;
- using their own prejudices to single out pupils – like a teacher who values athletes and finds a targeted pupil weedy;
- blaming the victim for being 'provocative';
- humiliating, degrading and undermining a pupil for their own amusement;
- laughing at the victim with the bullies.

Teachers who encourage bullying also protect themselves in case their victims or the parents of the victims complain about unfair treatment. They deflect criticism of their own actions by questioning the motives of the victim when they tell. They may say that the pupil produces substandard work or the pupil misunderstands the teacher's behaviour, or even that the pupil is paranoid and needs psychological help.

These teachers are bullies themselves and will infuriate you if you try to work with them or change their behaviour in any way. It is the job of the headteacher to do something about teachers like this. I feel there is no place in the teaching profession for them, unless they completely change their ways. The victims of these teachers feel distraught and have no place to turn for help. If you are a pupil and the adult is the problem, what can you do but start to believe it is your fault?

If you know a teacher who is acting like this, keep records, find out who knows and what they are doing about it, have a word with your headteacher and do not try to tackle the teacher alone about their behaviour. Be very careful in case the teacher decides to target you, because that is how they protect themselves. The only thing you cannot do is just ignore it. If the school ethos is such that the teacher holds sway and cannot be touched, you may have to find another job. Who wants to work in a school that harbours and protects teachers who encourage bullying and are bullies themselves? The consequences for you and for the school climate are overwhelming.

# The power of the positive

The young man who told me his story of the bullying teacher also said that another teacher took him under his wing and restored his self-confidence. 'That teacher made me feel great every time I saw him and I loved going to his class. He taught science and I eventually became a scientist because of him. He just made me feel I was OK.'

This young man told me the names of both teachers, but I will only tell you the name of the wonderful teacher, Mr Miller. Apparently he always found something positive to say.

---

**TOP TIPS!**

*Here are 10 things you can say to make pupils feel good:*

1 *You did that very well.*

2 *I admire the way you keep trying.*

3 *You have a good sense of humour.*

4 *I respect your opinion.*

5 *You have a real talent for ... art, music, sport, writing, maths, etc.*

6 *I appreciate your comments.*

7 *I saw how you helped that younger pupil and I was impressed.*

8 *I enjoy having you in my class.*

9 *You handled that situation very sensitively.*

10 *Thank you for being so positive.*

---

We all appreciate a compliment or kind word, and for your pupils and your fellow teachers a little praise goes a long way.

## Conclusion

After I wrote this I was reading a piece by a Sunday paper columnist who had just heard with great sadness about the death of her English teacher. She went on to write about how he encouraged her writing even when she was rejected in her early efforts to get published, how he made her laugh when she felt down or when someone made an unkind remark to her, and how she wished she had got back in touch with him to let him know how he had changed her life. Her comment that will stick with me is 'being a good teacher is a gift'. Here's to the Mr Millers of the teaching world: may we all be remembered as the teacher who made the difference.

### Going further

**Research on bullying**

Salmivalli, C., 'Participant role approach to school bullying: Implications for interventions', *Journal of Adolescence* 22 (1999): 453–9.

# Cyberbullying
## *Michele Elliott*

### What this chapter will explore:

- Types of cyberbullying
- How cyberbullying is different
- What teachers can do

Cyberbullying is using the internet, mobile phones or other technology to send or post images or text to harass, torment, harm or embarrass someone. It can include:

- threats;

- false statements designed to humiliate;

- ridicule in online forums;

- posing as the victim to attack others or to make the victim look foolish;
- setting up websites, posting rumours, sending instant messages and sending emails.

# Types of cyberbullying

Cyberbullying comes in many forms and by the time you read this there will probably be even more. Whenever technology moves forward, it seems the methods used to bully move with it. If you want to find out what is currently happening, ask your pupils. If you are teaching primary children, you may be surprised about how much some of them know about cyberbullying. I have heard of cases of children as young as eight getting together to send hateful texts on their mobiles.

### Why not try this?

Ask your pupils to come up with a definition of cyberbullying. With younger children, you may want to attach the idea to a lesson on bullying in general. Tell them you would like a simple explanation followed by examples. Later in this chapter there is a quiz that you can give pupils to help them decide if they have ever cyberbullied anyone or been victims or know anyone who has been. The purpose is for you to know what they know and to find out the latest trends.

Below is a summary of some of the main forms that cyberbullying takes.

## Websites

Pupils may create websites where they post photos, videos and information about the victim which might include their name, address and mobile phone number. They also mock up fake photos designed to humiliate and distress.

## Mobile phones

This common form of bullying includes sending abusive texts or video messages and photos. Cameras and videos in mobile phones allow pupils to take photos of other pupils in the gym taking a shower, or changing in the locker room, which they then post online or send to others. They can also set up fights and film the victims being hit, kicked, set on fire or having horrible stuff poured over them, and then send the images to others and post the results online. Bizarrely this has come to be called 'happy slapping'.

Groups of pupils may get together in what they call a text or warning war. They send hundreds of text messages to another pupil's mobile phone, resulting in great distress or even in the victim being kicked offline.

## Gaming

An example of how bullying moves with the times is interactive gaming. Interactive games allow pupils to communicate by live internet phone with others in a game online. Some players become abusive, using threats and bad language. They can also lock the victims out of the game and spread malicious rumours about them.

## Email

Using email, hate mail is sent to the victim, often by groups organised by the main bully. So pupils can get 50 emails saying that everyone hates them and that they should die. This, along with texts and hate websites, has resulted in some pupils committing suicide.

## Instant messenger/chatrooms

Here, messages are sent to the victim or to a group of pupils who then join in the 'conversation' to laugh at the victim.

## Internet ratings

Pupils may create a rating system in which they are asked to rank others in terms of looks or sexual attractiveness. They also poll pupils on questions like 'Who is the biggest slut in Year 9?' 'Who has the most zits?' 'Who is the thickest?', etc. Then they post the results for all to see.

## Social networks

Pupils sometimes set up profiles so that others can contribute to humiliate another pupil – or even a teacher. According to the Association of Teachers and Lecturers, 15 per cent of teachers surveyed had been targeted via cyberbullying (www.atl.org.uk). Bill Rogers talks about this kind of stress for teachers in his book *The Essential Guide to Managing Teacher Stress*.

It is relatively easy for pupils to get personal information or photographs and then use them on these networks to attack victims.

## Impersonation

Posing as the victim, a bully can post hateful or sexual messages or use a chatroom so that the other pupils think the victim has said these things. The bully posts the victim's name and address so that the victim is then inundated with comments from the angry chatroom group.

## Viruses

Hacking into another pupil's computer, deleting important information or sending a virus can destroy a computer or at least cause great inconvenience.

### Case study

Tyler had been at the same small village school for several years. He had no problems with the other children and was an excellent pupil. He had never been bullied and the school had quite effective anti-bullying policies. Then Tyler began to notice that some of his friends were acting strangely around him: they were laughing as he passed them, avoiding him at break and not contacting him as they had before. He found himself outside the group and had no idea why.

Tyler did not say anything to his parents but his teacher noticed that he seemed out of sorts and sat by himself at lunch. One of Tyler's teachers, Mr Adams, pulled him aside and asked if anything was troubling him. Tyler broke down and told him how confused he was by the treatment he was getting from other pupils for no apparent reason. Mr Adams made it his business to find out what was going on. He overheard (on purpose) pupils giggling about Tyler and eventually found out that they had set up a website and a blog about him. On the blog they had posted entries that Tyler had supposedly written, claiming he was gay and in love with a teacher. He was also quoted as saying how he hated certain pupils and the school and that he wanted to move. On the fake blog the pupils had Tyler accusing others of stealing his homework so that they could be as clever as he was.

Tyler was devastated to find that not one of his friends had come to him to tell him what was happening, though everyone seemed to know. Mr Adams followed the school's anti-bullying policy, called in the ringleaders one by one, and found out that one boy was secretly jealous of Tyler's intelligence and his popularity. That boy managed to get others to join him in his plot to undermine Tyler.

The parents of all the pupils were called in and appropriate sanctions given out to the culprits. The pupils apologised, took down as much of the online material as they could (once things are posted it is not always possible to retract them), and lessons were held on cyberbullying. This was a good school, but cyberbullying can happen right under the noses of the best teachers.

- How would you have handled this situation?
- What kind of support could be given to Tyler?
- How could you encourage your pupils to prevent this happening?
- What signs indicated that Tyler was having a problem?
- What would you do with the pupils who bullied Tyler to help them become more empathetic?

## TOP TIP!

*Watch out for pupils congregating around a computer or mobile phone, laughing and being secretive when they see you – it may be innocent, but it is worth investigating. Beware especially if one pupil seems to be excluded from this joviality.*

# How cyberbullying is different

Unlike other forms of bullying, using technology means bullies can be anonymous: by using fake names in chatrooms, instant messaging and pay as you go mobile phones, as well as by setting up temporary email accounts, websites, etc. This is bullying that allows the bullies to distance themselves from the torment they are causing. One girl told me that it was only a bit of fun – she never saw the enormous harm she did to her victim because there was no face-to-face conflict. Pupils say things they would never do in person. As one pupil said in a lesson, 'You might not go up to someone and say "'I think you're stupid and ugly'"', but over the internet you have the courage to do it because you don't have to see them look hurt.'

## TOP TIP!

*Remember that cyberbullying is never completely anonymous. Let pupils know that no matter how careful they are, their computer leaves a digital record that tells their service provider who they are. Most social networking sites tell people when they sign up that their site can be read and monitored. That means they can be tracked down, if necessary, through their Internet Protocol (IP).*

From the victim's viewpoint, there is no way to know how many people are out to get them. It could be one disgruntled ex-friend or everyone in the school. Because victims cannot identify who is bullying them, they don't know who to be wary of or how to respond. Cyberbullying makes pupils almost paranoid because they believe that not only are their classmates a threat, but that all those people who see what is online must also be laughing at them. One pupil described that he felt absolutely helpless.

It is almost impossible to oversee what is happening in cyberbullying because most online forums lack supervision. There are panic buttons installed in some programs and attempts by service providers to police offensive sites and individuals, but the reality is that once things are online, they can be seen by millions. Of course the victims know this and feel that everyone is against them.

If pupils are being bullied physically or verbally, they can retreat to their homes and feel safe for a while. Not so if they are being cyberbullied, because they can be harassed 24 hours a day, 7 days a week. Even if they avoid their computer, they can be texted on their mobile phone. And most pupils rely heavily on both, so to ask them to stop using these things is unfair and unrealistic. However, if a child is willing to forgo use of their mobile and computer, they can get away from the bullies. They can change their email address, mobile phone number and get safety filters that automatically bar certain senders.

That does not protect them against the defamatory images and text published online. Even if they are successful at getting the servers and networks to delete the offending material, once it is posted it can be downloaded, ensuring it can be reposted at any time. You can see why cyberbullying can be so overwhelming for its victims.

## Case study

Amelia (9) was a popular and intelligent girl – a leader within her group of girls. She never caused trouble until a new girl, Ruby, joined the class. Ruby was also bright and well-liked and was friends with all the girls, including Amelia. About half-way through the year, her teacher realised that Ruby was not the same happy girl and was starting to go downhill in her work. Amelia and the other girls continued to be a cohesive group, but Ruby seemed to be on the sidelines at playtime and she had lost her confidence.

Before the teacher had time to act, she got a call from Ruby's parents asking for a meeting. They came in the next day, bringing copies of the texts that the other girls in the class had sent to their daughter. There were about a hundred and they were all very nasty, including urging Ruby to jump in the river and drown and telling her she was ugly and smelled. Ruby had tearfully told her mother what had happened and the mother kept the messages, telling her daughter not to respond.

The teacher called in the girls one by one and found that Amelia had orchestrated the onslaught of hateful messages because she felt Ruby was taking over her position as top girl. The parents of all the girls involved were brought in, along with their child, and told what had happened. They agreed that the behaviour was appalling and handed out various punishments, such as no use of the computer or television and confiscation of mobile phones for a set time. That is, they all agreed except Amelia's parents, who tried to excuse her for spurious reasons. However, they came around in the end when shown the evidence.

The teacher changed the classroom seating, held lessons about cyberbullying and eventually the class gelled once more. In fact Amelia and Ruby became best friends – for now.

- How would you have dealt with Amelia and the other girls?
- How would you have supported Ruby?
- What would you say to the parents of Ruby?
- What would you say to the parents of the bullies?
- What would you do with the boys in the class, who were not involved but who knew what was happening?

# What teachers can do

## The school's role

Schools need anti-bullying policies and you are probably familiar with yours. Specifically, in relation to cyberbullying, you may wish to:

- evaluate with colleagues the effectiveness of your policy on cyberbullying – is it mentioned and prohibited?

- ensure that you and your colleagues are as up to date as possible;
- hold sessions for parents and liaise with them – you may have some IT parents who would be willing to advise about the latest safety ideas;
- find out about local help and initiatives;
- provide lessons and information for pupils.

There are government and charity sites that give you current information. Have a look at the list at the end of this chapter.

## Ethics

You can counteract cyberbullying most effectively if you have the time and resources to teach pupils about the ethics and even about the law in relation to cyberbullying. Although bullying itself is not a specific criminal offence, there are some laws about threatening behaviour or communications that could be applied. It is important for pupils to realise that there are consequences to putting things online, both ethically and legally. You could ask pupils to explore these possible consequences by reporting on cases in the media concerning law suits brought by victims of bullying, some of which have been successful (see www.childrenslegal centre.com).

### Why not try this?

Pupils can learn about online ethics and privacy by looking at their interactions and finding out that they are not as anonymous as they think they are.

Divide your pupils into small groups and ask them to draw a map of all online activities. Then ask which might put them at risk of cyberbullying. How should they react ethically if they have the opportunity to use the activity to bully another pupil? What should they do if they know someone is either a perpetrator or a victim of cyberbullying? What can bystanders do to make a difference?

As a class, look at all these possible areas of cyberbullying and see if it is possible to act more ethically in the virtual world. What are the implications if people do not act ethically? It might be useful to ask pupils to contrast how people act in the 'real' world with how many act online.

How might acting online now affect them in a few years? There have been several cases recently reported in the media in which young people have lost jobs because of what they have posted online. So if a pupil is not swayed by ethics, they could be influenced by the consequences of not acting ethically.

## TOP TIP!

One new teacher came up with the idea of suggesting to pupils that they think of someone they admired and/or respected and hoped to emulate. She asked pupils to use that person as a guide when deciding to do something online – a sort of 'virtual conscience'. The good thing about this idea is that you can use it with primary and secondary pupils for all kinds of discussion, not just cyberbullying.

## Why not try this?

Ask your pupils to devise a cyberbully quiz from the point of view of both bullies and victims. Here is a short example which might be useful.

| Have you ever: | Yes | No |
|---|:---:|:---:|
| 1  Known someone who has sent a nasty text but not told? | ☐ | ☐ |
| 2  Sent a text to someone deliberately to upset them? | ☐ | ☐ |
| 3  Set up a hate website about another pupil? | ☐ | ☐ |
| 4  Contributed a negative comment to a website about another pupil? | ☐ | ☐ |
| 5  Used your mobile to take photos of a bullying incident without intervening? | ☐ | ☐ |
| 6  Known a friend was cyberbullying but kept quiet? | ☐ | ☐ |
| 7  Laughed about someone being cyberbullied? | ☐ | ☐ |
| 8  Made fun of someone online or by email? | ☐ | ☐ |
| 9  Made a fake image and posted it to hurt someone? | ☐ | ☐ |
| 10  Bullied anyone using any form of technology? | ☐ | ☐ |

Give yourself 1 point for each yes, 0 for each no.

Scores:

0      You are an excellent role model – we wish we had more like you.

1–3    You need to stop this before you get worse.

4–6    You are hurting people and have a problem.

6–10  You are a cyberbully and need to change your behaviour now.

## Bystanders

As with all bullying, bystanders have a crucial role. Most pupils involved in cyber-bullying are going along with what is happening without really thinking about the implications for them and for the victims. You know the attitude: 'It was only a bit of fun.' The cyberbully needs an audience just as all bullies do, so ask your pupils to come up with suggestions about how bystanders can help stop cyberbullying. You could hold class discussions or use a quiz like the one on the previous page to get things going.

### Why not try this?

Another suggestion for teaching about cyberbullying is to have pupils make masks and hide behind them while talking to each other. This is fun in primary school and can be combined with art. The masks can be made out of papier mâché or just pieces of paper. Ensure that as much of the face as possible is covered so that expressions cannot be seen. Wear a mask yourself, if possible. Ask the pupils to imagine what it would be like if everyone wore a mask and you could not see if they were happy or sad or scared or angry. How would people know what anyone thought or felt? Would that be a good world to live in?

Relate this to the internet where people can say things and do things but cannot see how it affects others. What do you see if you bully someone in person? How is it different if you bully someone online? How does the person being bullied feel – online or in person? Does it matter that you cannot see how they feel?

You can keep and use the masks for future lessons or your pupils can take them home for discussions with parents. This is the kind of lesson that helps younger children understand about being anonymous online.

### TOP TIPS!

Here are 10 things pupils should know about cyberbullying:

1   Do not reply to abusive online or text messages.

2   If you continue to get abusive messages, do not open them.

3   If you can, keep copies of messages in a folder without opening them.

4   Do not give out personal information, like your name or phone number, online.

5   Use an alias online that does not give any information about you.

6  Only give your mobile number to trusted friends.

7  Contact your service provider if you continue to have problems.

8  Always tell a trusted adult if you are being cyberbullied.

9  Do not post anything online that might come back to haunt you later.

10  You are never completely anonymous online.

# Conclusion

Cyberbullying comes in multiple forms via social networks, mobiles, texts, blogs and websites – the list will only increase as more technologies become available. By letting pupils discuss the issues and quiz themselves, they will see whether they are standing up against cyberbullying or are perpetrating it. They also need to examine whether they are bystanders who allow cyberbullying to continue when they should take action.

The internet is a brilliant tool that can be used for good or ill. You need to learn as much as possible about the ways your pupils use the internet and then guide them about how to protect themselves from harm. If you can do that, plus foster a sense of responsibility about stopping cyberbullying, you've done well.

## Going further

**Useful websites**

www.atl.org.uk

www.bullying.co.uk

www.childnet-int.org

www.childrenslegalcentre.com

www.kidscape.org.uk

www.teachernet.gov.uk

**Book for teachers**

Rogers, B., *The Essential Guide to Managing Teacher Stress* (Pearson, 2010).

# Bullying in the early years

*Michele Elliott*

## What this chapter will explore:

- Can young children be bullies?
- Taking bullying seriously
- Practical ways to tackle young bullying
- Activities to use with young children

It is concerning that reception and infant teachers are experiencing an increase in the number of really nasty incidents from their young charges, including quite deliberate sustained bullying. As one teacher said: 'You expect the tantrums when pupils are learning to share and are uncertain about how they should act. But some of my pupils are embarking on

**campaigns of bullying that are frightening given their age.' This chapter looks more closely at bullying in the early years.**

# Can young children be bullies?

It may seem surprising that bullying should be an issue for young children, although you may have already found out from your own experience that it is. The anti-bullying charity Kidscape has recorded a large increase in the number of reported cases involving children aged 5 and under.

A father rang the Kidscape helpline to say that his 5-year-old daughter had been threatened in the playground by a boy wielding a knife! When he complained that the other child had been readmitted to the school after a brief suspension, he was told that the boy 'had family problems'. He was also 5 years old. Of course this was quite serious and might not be considered bullying. However, it turned out this boy had been bullying children since the age of 3.

We have also heard how the mother of a 4-year-old boy was in great distress after her son came home covered with mud and sporting a black eye. He had been set upon by a group of 5-year-olds and told that he better not tell or they would beat him up again the next day. Fortunately, the teacher in this case took immediate action and the bullying was nipped in the bud.

## Case study

One reception teacher told the parents of Sam (4) when they came to see her about bullying that 'it was only children playing – it wasn't bullying'. Yet Sam was being consistently punched and pushed by another child, Oliver. Oliver was also 4, but he knew he was hurting others; he only attacked when he thought no one was looking. He could control his behaviour and waited for the right moment to attack. He then denied he had done anything.

The bullied child, Sam, said he hated going to school and was wetting the bed again. Not surprisingly, he also started having difficulty outside school. His mother said that children in the neighbourhood picked on him and that he was becoming more and more timid.

The teacher re-evaluated what was happening when it became clear that Oliver was bullying other pupils besides Sam. She called in Oliver's parents and explained what he was doing and how often it was happening. Oliver's parents were not convinced their son was bullying, but they agreed that the teacher could set limits and not allow Oliver to get away with bad behaviour. Using a star chart, the teacher rewarded Oliver every time she found him being nice to another pupil and soon he was going out of his way to get stars. His parents agreed that when he brought home a full star chart they would give him a little treat – nothing grand but something like a small toy. Oliver is now doing well.

Sam needed his confidence boosting and the teacher and his parents found ways to praise him – for doing tasks, for learning new words, for reading aloud and even for smiling (he had been quite miserable). He started to come out of his shell and his parents started swimming lessons and playing ball games to help him feel better about himself. Sam is also doing well and he and Oliver even play together – a good result.

## Taking bullying seriously

If children as young as 3 or 4 might become victims and bullies, what can you do? Is it best to make a big fuss or to leave children to sort it out? More and more teachers say that bullying should be taken seriously and stopped from the earliest age. 'I used to just let the pupils sort it out themselves, but that was when the children were not so violent and the parents cooperated,' said one headteacher. 'Now we intervene immediately not only to stop injury but to prevent law suits.'

One teacher commented that the behaviour of children in her reception class had definitely changed over the past 15 years:

> Children are more likely now to lash out at each other and to act out violence in the playground than they were in the past. I am alarmed that some children deliberately bully others and cannot seem to understand the concept of kindness. If we don't stop them bullying now I think we are laying the foundations for short-term misery and later adult aggression. After all, versions of the playground heavies and their victims are re-enacted in sitting rooms and boardrooms daily.

### Why not try this?

Organise a 'Kindness Week'. Ask your pupils to draw pictures about how they can be kind to others. Give prizes for the best kindness ideas, and ribbons or certificates for pupils being kind to others. You could also give children badges and happy-faces stickers. Involve parents, if possible.

→

You may need to explain kindness. You could use pictures of baby animal pets and ask how they would be kind to the animal – for example, holding it carefully, stroking it gently, feeding it or playing nicely with it. You can then ask what would not be kind – for example, hurting it, starving it or hitting it. Apply this concept to people by asking if it is kind to hit someone, or push them down or call them names. That is not being kind. Being kind is sharing, allowing others to play games together and saying good things about others.

It is common sense that tackling bullying issues with young children should eliminate a lot of problems for them as they grow up – both for victims and for bullies. To do this, we need to understand who are the bullies and who are the victims.

## Who are the bullies?

Probably all young children bully once in a while – brother and sisters, if no one else. Young children may also be so intent on getting what they want that they just bowl over anyone in their way. Most children do not even realise that they are harming someone. Or a young child may go along with the crowd and say or do hurtful things without thinking through what they are doing.

While all pupils need to learn to get along with others, concern about young bullies should be focused more on the pupil who deliberately sets out to cause distress to another pupil or who is a danger to other young pupils. These are the children who have problems and may share the characteristics outlined in Chapter 1 of this book.

## Who are the victims?

The under-5s who become victims of bullying are described by their teachers as sensitive, gentle children. They are not used to conflict, so when bullies come at them they do not know what to do. They frequently ask why someone would want to bully them – they've done nothing to deserve it and they have not been treated this way before. The sad fact is that, from the bully's viewpoint, these gentle children make excellent targets because they are nice and won't fight back. If you could point out one 'fault' of these victims, it would be that they are too nice! However, in a school, nursery or playgroup that does not tolerate bullying, they should have no problems.

Yet there are some children who seem to get bullied everywhere – at school, parties, activities, the local playground – you name it and they are bullied. These are the children who seem almost to thrive on the negative attention they get when they are bullied. It is as if the bullying confirms their opinions of themselves that they are worthless and deserve what is happening to them. There may be problems in the lives of these children or they may have been bullied right from the day when they started nursery school and never recovered their confidence.

# Practical ways to tackle young bullying

## Why not try this?

There are many practical ways in which you can prevent young bullying. Here are a few that have been successfully used by teachers:

- Decorate your classroom with images of friendship and cooperation.

- Read stories about children helping each other (see the end of this chapter for some books on bullying and friendship).

- Explain what bullying is – i.e. when a child hurts another child on purpose or says mean things – and make it clear that your school does not allow bullying.

- Explain to your class that this is a school where children tell if they are being picked on.

- Tell your pupils that they should tell you if they are being bullied or if they see bullying happening.

- Explain what will happen if pupils bully, as detailed in your anti-bullying policy – for example, time out, or eating lunch alone, or missing out on playtime, etc.

- Ensure that you do something if you are told. Children must be able to rely on a sympathetic and helpful response if they do tell: in this way they learn that speaking out will make things better, while keeping quiet will make things worse.

- Constantly monitor the trouble spots, for example the playground. If lack of staff is a problem (where isn't it?), enlist parent helpers.

- Let other staff members know if you are concerned about a particular child and ask them to help observe and intervene if necessary.

- Use lessons, activities and art projects to reinforce the anti-bullying message (see pages 61–3 for ideas).

- Put up a photograph of each child and write something positive about them under the photo. Try just a few words like: 'A good friend' or 'Helps others' or 'Kind person' or 'Good to pets'. Change the words  →

once a week and ask the children to help think of good things about each other.

- Give stickers or rewards of some sort to a child who has been nice (sometimes it is difficult to 'catch' a problem child being nice, but it is worth the effort to reinforce good behaviour). Children will vie to be good if they get recognition. Make sure that every child gets recognised at some point.

## Set up student helpers

The idea of using students to help others is as old as teaching itself. I used student helpers when I taught in a school that had pupils aged 3 to 11. This gave me a pool of older pupils to help prevent younger ones being picked on. This is a more low-level approach than setting up peer mentoring schemes like those in Chapter 11, but it can be worth assigning an older buddy or helper to act as an adviser, protector and mentor to each new child. Usually older or bigger pupils pick on younger or smaller ones *who are alone*. If the younger pupils are with older pupils, it eliminates that problem and you may find that older pupils take pride in helping 'their' charges.

## Help the bully

Sometimes it is possible to help bullies by recognising that they, too, are victims; perhaps unloved or mistreated at home, or covering for a feeling of personal inadequacy by dominating others. In these cases, treating the underlying cause may also eradicate the bullying. For instance, if a child who is doing badly is encouraged to work hard and excel at something – for example, drawing, gymnastics, plasticine modelling, using a skipping rope, putting together puzzles, racing, etc. – they may in the process gain enough approval to stop bullying. The younger the child, the better chance you have of changing their behaviour.

### Why not try this?

Here are some practical ways to help when working with a young child who is bullying:

- Take immediate action – which may involve separating the child who is bullying from other children.
- Talk to the child to find out if they are upset or have been bullied and are lashing out as a reaction.

- Find out if the child realises that they are bullying and hurting someone else – sometimes young children do not know how their actions affect others,

- Use previously agreed sanctions, such as five minutes of 'time out'.

- Talk with the parents of the victim, if possible, to set things right and to avoid the bullying carrying on.

- Set up a behaviour chart using stars or stickers – give a reward for every five or ten stars. However, make sure that the time between the good behaviour and the reward is not too great, especially for very young children – for example, some children may need help every 10 minutes to behave while others can go for a day.

## TOP TIP!

*Make sure the play area has places to play enthusiastically, to play with balls and toys or games, and to play quietly. This avoids pupils running into each other and any ensuing problems.*

## Why not try this?

If the parents of a bully ask for advice from you, encourage them to follow these suggestions:

- Work with you to figure out the best way to help their child.

- Talk to their child and explain that, whatever problems there may be, bullying is not the way to solve them.

- Work out a 'behaviour plan' and reward good behaviour.

- Arrange a daily or weekly report from you to them, and vice versa.

- Set up a star chart on the refrigerator and give a star for each good report from you, followed by some sort of reward after so many stars.

- Explore counselling or professional help if the child does not respond after a reasonable time – the child may have problems that need to be sorted out before they can stop bullying.

## Help the victims

Some bullies, especially young ones who receive help, can be sorted out. However, we have to work around bullies by teaching children how to cope with threats and how to avoid attracting them in the first place. Some children may seem more prone to bullying than others. This may result from factors beyond their control, which set them apart from others and that the bully decides to pick on: the colour of their skin, for example, or some striking physical feature, such as being above or below average height or having a disability or some deformity. Often children are bullied because the bully is looking for someone to pick on because the bully has problems, but if a child is repeatedly bullied – for whatever reason – then they might take on a victim mentality. If this happens, you can help them.

### Why not try this?

Try practising the following with victims of bullying:

- Walk tall and straight, in a confident way, rather than hunched over, looking scared and uncertain.

- Look in the mirror and say 'No' or 'Leave me alone' in a clear, loud voice. Young children especially seem to enjoy doing this and it really works because a firm rebuff often puts off a bully.

- Act out the threatening situation, responding calmly but firmly. This type of imaginative play can also help defuse some of the anger that builds up inside children who are persistently bullied.

- Ignore the bullying and pretend not to be upset – turn and walk quickly away and tell a grown-up.

- Use humour and laughter – it is more difficult to bully a child who refuses to take the bullying seriously.

- Respond to taunts by saying the same thing over and over. For example, with a taunt such as 'You're ugly', a response such 'Thank you' is ridiculous but effective if you just keep saying it over and over – 'Thank you, thank you.' It is silly and has nothing to do with what the bully is saying, but it becomes boring for the bully after a while.

### TOP TIP!

Practice is the key. For children to feel confident with these ideas, practise with them and see if they can come up with other ideas. Obviously the ability of the child to try these things depends upon their age and maturity.

## Why not try this?

You can also help children develop confidence by:

- assuring them that the bullying is not their fault;
- telling the child that you like them (bullied children feel they are unlovable);
- helping pupils to stop any bad habits that might be contributing to their being bullied (such as picking their nose, or wiping disgusting things on their sleeves, or grabbing toys from other children).

If a child continues to be bullied, it may be that counselling would help. Like the bully, the chronic victim and their family may need some professional guidance to prevent the child from becoming a life-long victim.

# Activities to use with young children

The good news is that most of your young pupils will not suffer bullying, but they will benefit from learning about how bullying is wrong and why it is better to be friendly than to be nasty. So included here are many activities that early years teachers have shared and which you might enjoy using.

## Rip-Rip

Give each child a large cut-out figure of a child, made from A3 paper (or smaller if necessary). Explain that the 'child' is a whole, happy person who is going to school one morning feeling good. But during the day other children make comments or do things that make the child feel bad. Ask the children to make a little rip in their cut-out figure every time they think the figure is hurt by something in the story you are going to read out:

*I can't wait to get to school. I know it's going to be fun. Oh, look, here come some other kids.*

*'Hello, my name is Jane. What's yours?'*

*What are they saying to me? They said I was ugly and they wouldn't speak to me. (Rip-Rip)*

*Here come some other children. Maybe they'll be friendlier. What are they doing? Oh, they're looking away and pretending not to hear the mean children calling me names. I wish they would do something. I feel so lonely. (Rip-Rip)*

*I guess I'll just play by myself today.* (Rip-Rip)

*In the playground some of the children wait until no one is looking and then they trip me over. One of them says not to tell or I'll be in trouble. I don't tell.* (Rip-Rip)

*No one will sit by me at lunch. The mean children have told them not to talk to me or eat with me.* (Rip-Rip)

*When my mummy comes to collect me, she asks me if school was fun today. What should I tell her?*

You can make up your own story or add or subtract from this one. The children's figures will be in shreds by now. Discuss with them how it feels to be picked on like this and how they could have helped the cut-out child. Make a list of their suggestions and post it up in the class. Remind them how comments and actions can affect people, and encourage them to make kind comments to each other.

## That's my potato!

Give each child a potato and ask them to look at it carefully to see things like green marks, spots, its shape, 'eyes', etc. Try to ensure that the potatoes are not completely uniform! Ask the children to give their potato a name and make up a story about it. For example:

- What does it do for fun?
- What kinds of food does it like and dislike?
- How old is it?
- Does it have brothers and sisters?

Have the children tell their potato story to each other in small groups, or to you if you have enough time and not too many children. Then put all the potatoes in a bag, jumble them up and put them on a table for the children to come and find their potato. (If the children are likely to disagree, you will have to put a dot or some mark to avoid arguments.)

Explain that it is the small differences that make people individual but they are still all people, just as the potatoes may each be different but they are all still potatoes. Once you take the time to look at someone and really get to know them, you can see that no person is the same as anyone else and that differences are no reason to bully anyone. After all, just because their potato may have three 'eyes' and someone else's potato may have six 'eyes', does that mean that their potato should be singled out for bad treatment?

## Drawings

Ask the children to draw a picture of a playground where everyone is happy and no one is being bullied. Then ask for a picture of a playground where children are being bullied. Use the pictures to have a discussion about bullying. You can make the pictures into a wall mural.

## Puppets

Use puppets to help young children understand how to be kind. Act out a scene in which one puppet is mean to another, and ask the children to make the nasty puppet say or do something nice.

## Songs

You may have a genius for music – if so, make up simple songs about friends and being kind. Or find songs with friendship themes or make up new words to songs like 'Twinkle twinkle little star'. It can go something like:

*Friendly, friendly little star,*

*How I wonder where you are.*

*You are kind to everyone,*

*That is why you are such fun.*

You will be better at coming up with words, but speaking of stars ...

## Lonely star

Cut out a star and use it to tell the story of a lonely little star that has no friends. Ask the children how they could help the lonely star. Usually they will talk about having other stars for friends and you can ask them to draw lots of stars. Put the lonely star up with all the children's stars around it and talk about how lovely it is to help the lonely star. You know where this is going ... relate it to children and how it is good to feel that children are trying to be friendly to others.

# Conclusion

The one thing that emerges time and time again in all surveys is that bullying is one of the most difficult social problems children have to deal with, especially as they get older and the methods of bullying become more sophisticated. At least most of the children you are dealing with are not setting up hate websites or using social networking or mobile phones to bully other young children – I hope. But they are getting important messages about how to behave and what you expect. Regardless of what is being taught to them at home, you can make a huge difference by tackling bullying behaviour.

## Going further

**Useful website**

www.kidscape.org.uk

(see downloads: 'Don't Bully Me!' and 'Keeping Young Children Safe')

**Books for 3–5-year olds**

Damjan, M., *Big Squirrel and Little Rhinoceros* (Pavilion, 2009).

Dodd, L., *Scarface Claw* (Puffin, 2009).

Elliott, M., *Feeling Happy, Feeling Safe* (Hodder, 1991).

Jennings, L., *Fred* (Little Tiger Press, 1996).

McCaferty, J. and Roxbee Cox, P., *Don't Be a Bully, Billy* (Usborne, 2004).

Rosen, M., *Little Rabbit Foo Foo* (Walker Books, 2003).

Ross, T., *Is It Because?* (Andersen Press, 2006).

Simon, F., *Hugo and the Bully Frogs* (Gullane Children's Books, 2005).

Thomas, J., *Can I Play?* (Egmont Books, 2003).

Van Genechten, G., *Flop-Ear and His Friends* (Cat's Whiskers, 2005).

# A primary school approach
## *Linda Frost*

**What this chapter will explore:**

- The school's attitude to bullying
- Identifying bullying in primary schools
- Peer groups
- Solutions to bullying

Defining bullying is important (see Chapter 1), but far more important is how a school puts its anti-bullying policy into practice. This chapter looks at some of the issues you may want to consider when setting up and implementing an anti-bullying policy in primary schools.

# The school's attitude to bullying

## Draconian or understanding?

It is more helpful to have a 'draconian' anti-bullying policy that sets out definite actions rather than an 'understanding' policy that is vague and depends upon interpretation. Young pupils respond better when they know exactly what will happen and why.

That does not mean you have to resort to any of your sanctions, but it is very helpful to have them there if a severe situation occurs. My headteacher colleagues sometimes worry that it might put off parents if they see that a policy includes detention or pupils missing school journeys as possible sanctions. But it won't affect your recruitment: the majority of parents are happy to know that bullies are going to be dealt with, and parents of bullies seldom believe their child falls into a bully category anyway!

In one school, a pupil kicked another so badly that he broke the victim's leg. The school's anti-bullying policy did not state that any pupil could be *excluded* for such behaviour. When the pupil was excluded it was overturned in a legal challenge as 'not being stated as a sanction in the school policy'. This is why you need to put in enough contingencies to cover even extreme situations.

## Teasing or bullying?

You may hear from pupils and parents that a bullying incident was really just kids being kids and teasing each other. Yet the pupils who are being 'teased' tell you that they are upset and the teasing feels like bullying. It's true that everyone gets a bit of good-natured and mutual teasing once in a while – that is healthy, and some pupils may need help in learning a bit of give and take. But sometimes you need to be able to determine if what is happening is just teasing or is really bullying (see Figure 6.1). In some schools teasing is banned, but that seems unrealistic.

> ### Why not try this?
>
> Say to your pupils that it is sometimes hard to know if someone is being a bully or just trying to do something they think is funny. Here are some questions pupils can ask themselves:
>
> - Is what I am saying or doing hurting the other person's feelings?
> - Would I want someone to say or do that to me?
> - Am I angry about something and taking it out on someone else?

- Has someone hurt my feelings and am I trying to get even?
- Am I making someone afraid because of what I am saying or doing?
- Do I chase or frighten younger pupils?
- Do I make fun of someone's looks or clothes or family?

Ask them to come up with other questions or ask them to draw a picture based on the theme of not hurting someone else. For example, the picture can show pupils being nice or saying something nice.

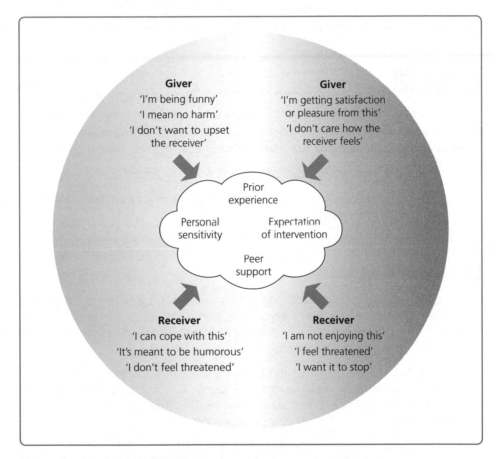

**Figure 6.1:** Teasing or bullying?
*Source:* Kidscape

# Identifying bullying in primary schools

You can find out what your pupils are experiencing by giving them a survey or questionnaire (see also Chapter 13). I conducted a survey with a new Year 3 intake two weeks after they had started in the junior department. Over half felt they had been bullied in their first two weeks. They also made it clear who they thought the bullies were.

What was interesting was the way these pupils then classified the pupils they thought were bullies. Three months later, I found that once pupils had identified someone as a bully, the impression remained very strong, even if it was not reinforced by subsequent experience. Any further interaction involving that pupil was viewed negatively; hence the bullying persisted in the victim's mind. This was not always fair, so we used discussion, drawings and posters to gradually change the climate into one of trust.

## TOP TIP!

*If you use a survey or questionnaire, ask specific questions to cover each aspect of bullying behaviour, and apply a limited time scale. For example, since the start of this school year, has anyone:*

- *physically hurt you enough to leave a mark or bruise?*
- *made comments that upset you so much that you couldn't sleep or didn't want to come to school the next day?*

## Bully/victim overlap

I also asked pupils, in confidence, to identify pupils they believed to be very powerful bullies. Four or five names reappeared continuously, and this was mirrored in responses from pupils throughout the school, even though these people were not always identified as a problem by teachers.

There were factors that many of the bullies and victims shared – an overlap of characteristics between bullies and victims. I found that both groups had low self-esteem, or had been bullied themselves. Many bullies felt they were victims, not bullies, and consequently felt unfairly picked upon.

Both groups often mirrored behaviour they had learned as responses from their home environment. Both groups had been defined by their choice of response when faced with challenging situations. They made either a:

- **passive response** – to back down (You're OK, I'm not OK); or an
- **aggressive response** – to attack back (I'm OK, you're not OK).

But they seldom seemed to use the more helpful:

● **assertive response** – to hold their ground but give a balanced response (I'm OK – and so are you).

## Bystanders

Bystanders are discussed in Chapter 1, but it is worth reiterating that they are crucial to every interaction. It is the role of the bystander that can change the power balance in a confrontational situation.

If bystanders feel safe and secure in their environment, they can intervene and support the victim. If they don't feel that it is personally safe to do so, they have a responsibility to report the incident to a teacher. What is not acceptable is that the bystander does nothing to help, or through fear, boredom or voyeurism exacerbates the situation by encouraging the bully.

If you can work on the self-esteem of all your pupils, you may find the bystanders blocking the bullies and the victims being supported.

### Why not try this?

Raise everyone's self-esteem by having a 'Positive Week'.

Leave a pile of slips of paper by the class post-box. They can say different things, such as:

● I'd like to thank ... because ...

● What I like most about ... is ...

● I trust ... as a friend because ...

● ... is someone I admire because ...

Ask the pupils to fill in a form for a classmate any time someone does a kindness, or behaves in a way that they find impressive. Share their feedback with each pupil at the end of the week. (You might want to screen these before sharing, so that any 'insensitive' comments are moderated, or so that everyone has received at least one positive message!)

# Peer groups

Pupils don't start from a level playing field. Some are carefree, others are sensitive, but each has skills that can be utilised. It's only 'human' that occasionally you find one particular child's behaviour challenging, irritating – or just totally impossible! By looking at the child's role in the peer group, it is possible to understand and support them more effectively.

Here are outlines of characteristics for each group.

## Sages

One of the interesting factors to emerge from the pupil survey mentioned earlier was that there was a small group who said they had never been bullied. These were pupils whose demeanour, behaviour and attitude exempted them from harassment. I nicknamed this group the 'sages'. They were usually intelligent, non-contentious, seen by other pupils as fair and generally held in high esteem by their peer group.

**TOP TIP!**

*Make sages your peer mentors!*

## Outsiders

Another group I called the 'outsiders'. These shared some characteristics with the sages, but were mainly pupils who 'didn't need anyone', and to a great extent they remained uninvolved in the group dynamics. These pupils tended to go their own way and had little effect on their peers, either positive or negative.

**TOP TIP!**

*It helps all involved if you team an outsider with a pupil who has been excluded from a larger peer group.*

## Victims or targets

Another group comprised the 'victims' or, as I prefer to call them, 'targets'. Often they were pupils of low prestige within the group and were seen as misfits. Some of these pupils almost seemed to invite bullying, by compliance rather than aggression, or by being thoroughly irritating. They had low self-esteem and would cry or stamp their feet, but would not ask for support. They therefore offered all the excitement of an anguished victim with no fear of repercussions. I asked one pupil who was identified as a victim why she did not ask for help when bullied. She responded: 'Bullied? I don't get bullied. It was much worse at my last school. It's better here.'

**TOP TIP!**

*Some assertiveness training would really help this group – preferably before they reach the point where they are ostracised by everyone!*

## Provocative victims

There was another group of pupils who seemed to encourage bullying behaviour as a form of attention seeking. For example, one pupil persistently stood in the playground goal mouth, where he was continually jostled and hit with the football. This meant he could get individual attention and first aid on a regular basis. For these pupils, any attention is better than none. It also reinforces their self-image of being a 'loner' or 'of little worth'.

**TOP TIP!**

*Set up star charts or achievement records that reward those pupils for positive behaviour, and try to avoid rewarding attention-seeking strategies.*

## Bullies

In this survey, it was often difficult to pick the pupils identified as bullies. They were not necessarily the biggest or strongest and had no clearly defined ranking in the peer group. Some were respected or feared; some had physical or other skills that were admired. One group was made up of outcasts who only managed to keep friends by manipulation or threats and were socially isolated in terms of real friends. Often, like their victims, they suffered from low self-esteem. They saw an aggressive role as one necessary for survival, and had built upon power to reinforce their prestige.

**TOP TIP!**

*These pupils often have low self-esteem too, so treat as you would victims.*

## Secret bullies

Another group was a surprise. Their behaviour towards adults was different from their private response to peers. They gave the impression of being class leaders – the most popular pupil in the class. In effect, their dominance was accepted, and the response of the other pupils was to appease or 'keep on the right side of them'. Such pupils came to expect that others would carry their coats and books or share their belongings to remain in favour. They were often seen as 'future leaders' or 'admirable for their strength of character' by adults.

> ### TOP TIP!
>
> *Keep a careful eye on these pupils, and don't allow them too much unsupervised power.*

A thorough knowledge of the dynamics of the many groups involved in schools, especially from the viewpoint of pupils, can therefore be highly enlightening, and helpful when planning effective strategies like supervising pupils around school.

> ### Why not try this?
>
> Young children love the idea of badges – like Blue Peter badges. Why not make badges that pupils can wear when they are especially kind or helpful to others? The badges could say 'Star pupil' or 'Helper' or just be a smiley face, but you will find that once some pupils have them, they will all want one. It can be good way to bring acting-out pupils into line in a positive way.

# Solutions to bullying

## Supervision and observation

Bullying flourishes where supervision is minimal. Travelling to school and leaving at the end of the day, lunch breaks, playtimes, moving between classes and 'playing out' after school and at weekends all afford the bully the best opportunities.

> ### Why not try this?
>
> Draw up a plan of the school (see Figure 6.2). Then ask meals or playground supervisors to mark the location of any act of bullying with an X on the plan

for a period of one week. The outcomes may be predictable, but will reinforce the need for supervisors to be strategically placed with areas of individual responsibility.

You can ask the pupils to do the same – they will show up places you did not even consider to be key areas, and perhaps suggest how your 'sage' pupils can help by being around those areas.

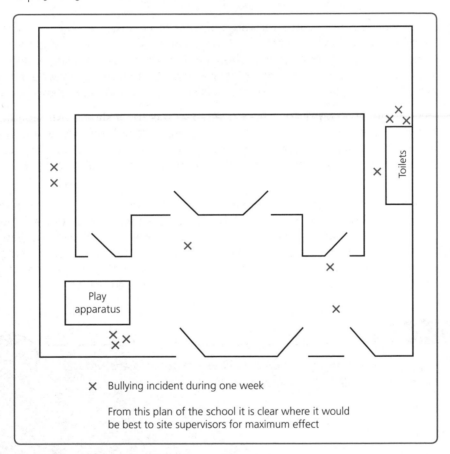

X    Bullying incident during one week

From this plan of the school it is clear where it would be best to site supervisors for maximum effect

**Figure 6.2:** Plan of the school showing incidents of bullying

I decided to take a video camera (or you can use your mobile to do the same thing) around to these areas during a lunch break. I made sure the pupils saw what I was doing. Surprise, surprise! Smiling pupils walked in gentile fashion to the stairs without the customary pushing. Huddled groups behind the play apparatus and out of sight in the toilet entrance melted away as soon as the camera approached. This also let the pupils know that I knew where to look for bullying. It reduced the rate of bullying incidents in those areas immediately.

**TOP TIP!**

*Try installing a CCTV camera in an identified bullying area. It doesn't matter whether the camera works or not – it will have the same effect of moderating undesirable behaviour (some fake ones even have battery-operated little red flashing lights).*

Merely observing a bully when they are unaware of being watched can identify the number of negative contacts made in a very short period. Sometimes a doubting parent may come into the school without their child knowing and look at their child at play for half an hour. Most parents are often totally amazed at the behaviour of their 'little angel', and more willing then to cooperate to improve it.

In a 45-minute lunch break, one father witnessed his son instigate five separate unprovoked incidents involving taunting, tripping, barging and threatening. By the end of the break, the father was groaning with embarrassment and far more willing than before to support the school in a behaviour modification programme for his son.

A mother who told me that her daughter would never be cruel to another pupil was extremely cooperative after seeing her child repeatedly freeze out another girl from the group. The victim in this case had been left out of birthday party invitations on the instructions of this girl. The mother, to her credit, ensured her daughter became a much nicer person. By the time she left to go to secondary school, the girl was a positive leader – and I was sorry to see her go.

**TOP TIP!**

*Be aware of the group of pupils in your school who are most vulnerable to bullying. For example, pupils with:*

- *dyspraxia*
- *dyslexia*
- *autistic spectrum disorder*
- *red hair!*

*It is not their fault they have any of these things and in fact most pupils who are bullied have nothing different about them in any way. The bottom line is that the bully has a problem and seeks out a victim, who may also be vulnerable in some way.*

## Parental support

Parental support is crucial (see Chapter 10). Sometimes pupils feel their parents will be more impressed if they can 'stand up for themselves'. Living up to a tough image to impress people who matter can be just as precarious and stressful as waiting for the next round of bullying to start.

Alternatively, other parents have raised their children with the philosophy to 'be nice to everyone, and they'll be nice to you'. Unfortunately they soon find that not all families share this viewpoint, and then they and their children are unprepared for dealing with unprovoked aggression from others.

Whatever the parent's view, if you can get them involved then it is easier to deal with helping both the bully and the victim.

### TOP TIP!

*Sadly, the problems for nice pupils is compounded if the response from the school is to blame the victim rather than dealing with the bully. Try not to use comments such as:*

- *'Your child needs to toughen up, they're too sensitive.'*
- *'Maybe your child needs counselling/a special needs assessment.'*
- *'Your child can stay in the library every break.' (While the bully goes unchecked.)*

## Readjusting class balances

When looking at your written school polices, may I strongly suggest that you include the following clause:

> We reserve the right to readjust the balance of classes at the end of each year by moving pupils, if we feel this is beneficial to the whole-school community.

Why? Because bullying by groups of pupils may mean you need to change pupils around. In fact 'power groups' of pupils should be split up regularly if possible. The parents of bullies are those most likely to protest if you want to move their child, and often it is the poor victim who is moved instead. This is unfair because the victim, already suffering with low self-esteem, has to try to create new friendship groups in an established class. If you can move several pupils it reduces the power base of the bullies, which is also good for them. This clause keeps the school's options open!

## Positive code of behaviour

Pupils should be encouraged to share in the responsibility for the safety and well-being of each other. You can ask your class to participate in drawing up an acceptable code of behaviour that emphasises the 'dos' rather than the 'don'ts'. The overall message should be quite simple:

*Pupils have a right to feel safe and supported in school.*

It is best to help pupils learn to recognise when they are about to violate this right, and they should be allowed 'time out' to cool down, perhaps in a time-out room if you have space for one, and to ask for help to resolve the difficulty.

## Suspension

However, the negative side of this is that pupils who cannot control themselves, and who are consistently guilty of premeditated attacks or violent revenge over long-held grudges, should be suspended for the protection of all the pupils. Schools should outline clear boundaries, as well as programmes for working with pupils who are victims or bullies.

## Clear boundaries

All pupils need the support of firm, clearly explained boundaries, but extreme measures should not be used in isolation, or as a 'knee-jerk' reaction to a situation. It is vital to build up an ongoing picture of the pupil's behaviour patterns, keeping in close contact with the parents to try to establish reasons for the problems and seeking ways of moderating their negative effects. Rewarding good behaviour is part of this, but preferably in an individual plan. Nothing is more demoralising for a pupil than to see a bully constantly receiving a stream of awards for minimal effort while their continual efforts to achieve go unrewarded. Passive and vulnerable pupils end up feeling like 'wallpaper' in this situation.

Pupils may turn to bullying when weighed down with anger, or highly stressed by some external social factor. Identifying with a trusted adult may be all that is needed. If the parents are willing to cooperate at an early stage, then a two-way diary, stressing the pupil's positive achievements at home and school, may be adequate to raise self-esteem and counter those feelings of persecution that start the spiral of negative behaviour.

## Telling

Pupils should be strongly encouraged to think of 'telling' as positive, not as 'grassing'. Bullies must not be allowed to maintain a conspiracy of silence and they need to realise they cannot single out victims without others knowing what is happening.

Unfortunately, one of the difficulties that can result from 'telling' is retaliation. When you intervene to protect a victim, unless the sanction is very powerful it will only be effective for as long as the situation continues to be closely monitored. As soon as the bully sees an opportunity, they may be tempted to seek revenge. The victim is then in an even more vulnerable position and dependent on remaining near a protecting adult for safety. The victim has therefore sacrificed freedom of movement for what might be temporary sanctuary, unless we ensure that the whole school is safe for all pupils. Even then you cannot protect pupils all the time. One cheeky pupil said:

'Miss, if I kick him will you suspend me?'

'Yes!'

'But what can you do if I leave him alone in school, but get him when he's in the park on Sunday afternoon?'

Nothing, is probably the answer, but at least you can ensure that in school the victim is safe and that the bully may have to have their freedom restricted. It may not solve the long-term problem but it will provide much-needed boundaries for the bully and relative safety for the victim.

## TOP TIP!

*Don't expect a frightened pupil to identify a bully in front of their peers. They will just stop telling you when they have a problem.*
*Give pupils a private way to let you know they are being bullied, such as permission to send you a note or email, after which you find a safe place to talk.*

## Why not try this?

You and your vulnerable pupil can establish a 'safe word' as a confidential alert when they feel worried and want some confidential support. For example, one pupil came up with the word 'guitar'. So when he was being harassed, he said that he was hoping to take guitar lessons after school. His teacher knew he wanted to talk and arranged a safe time. You will only want to do this with a limited number of pupils or you will go crazy trying to remember which word fits which pupil!

## Listening

Positive listening is essential. Don't finish your pupil's sentence to save time. If you are busy, tell them it is important but you need to arrange a suitable time when you will not be interrupted. Spending two minutes listening now may save a day of distress and lost learning.

### TOP TIPS!

- *Hold eye contact throughout.*
- *Repeat the substance of the problem back to the pupil at the end of the conversation.*
- *Take notes if it helps.*

### Reflecting on practice

Mohamed was a Year 3 pupil who had recently moved to a new school. He immediately became a target because the school had a culture of bullying and the bullies were delighted with a fresh victim. The teacher in this case came down hard on the bullies, but the school ethos did not support her.

If you are in such a situation you may find that:

- The bully's interpretation of your actions is that you are the biggest bully of all.
- Pupils see bullying as endemic, rather like the common cold – there's no known cure, so they put up with it and hope it goes away soon.
- Bullying becomes a cheap spectator sport – promoting the 'cheer it on and be glad it's not you' mentality.
- Often the instigator is the brighter pupil who stays out of trouble, but winds up someone with a short temper and then stands back to enjoy the show. Sometimes this kind of intelligence can be turned round to work positively to protect the more vulnerable class members by ensuring that the instigator is trained to take on a helper role instead (see Chapter 11).

Eventually Mohamed's parents moved him and he had a happy school experience. The ethos of that school only changed when a new headteacher came in with a new broom and involved the pupils to defeat the apathy.

## Peer group pressure

The most effective solution to bullying problems must be peer group pressure. Pupils should be empowered, with the support of teachers, to be accountable and responsible. This utilises the key groups identified earlier: the sages, outsiders, victims and bullies.

If pupils are given a forum such as circle time, class meetings or assemblies – or whatever you wish to call it – they will be able to identify and debate anti-social behaviour. This allows every pupil to assume the role of protector. Looking at the peer groups earlier in this chapter it is probable that:

- Sages will assume the role of advocate and improve their perceived status still further.
- Outsiders will be drawn in as impartial observers.
- Victims will become the focus of everyone's concern and support.
- Bullies will see the balance of power shifting away from them and their opportunities for retaliation diminished.

In a situation where pupils are regularly given the opportunity to discuss issues and change practice, they feel empowered and respond more readily to the need for social responsibility in a wider context.

Given this forum from a young age, children feel part of the justice system, not just passive recipients. Even 5-year-olds can embrace this – ours did and were wonderfully honest most of the time. Developing skills for citizenship must start at the earliest possible age to ensure that the ethos of a pupil's right to be heard when they have a problem or feel strongly about an issue will be firmly established within the school philosophy.

# Conclusion

We must look at the problem of bullying in primary schools dispassionately and deal with it in partnership with parents, encouraging pupils to be confident and feel supported as they grow into responsible, empowered citizens. Basically we are teaching good citizenship skills. There is a climate of concern about violence and anti-social behaviour in our schools. The problem can be addressed by employing preventative strategies (see Chapter 12), such as assertiveness training programmes, an effective whole-school anti-bullying policy, two-way involvement with parents, the acceptance of telling and sharing problems, and encouraging pupils to have a sense of communal responsibility. The insidious bullying that affects so many pupils will then be undermined and considered an anathema, and a more responsible, positive set of social values will be established as the norm for all pupils. We should all aspire to teach in this kind of school.

# Sample forms

To keep on top of what is happening, you may wish to use forms like those below, or adapt them to a computer program. Gathering information like this allows you to be proactive and to be able to predict where you need to be on your walks around the school. It helps you to see what is happening, rather than always putting pressure on the victim to report incidents.

You may want to colour-code this information for easy access (for example, behaviour reports could be orange and parent interviews bright blue). These reports help to establish any pattern (for example, playground behaviour being significantly worse after a weekend) and also chart if a pupil's misbehaviour varies according to the approach, status or attitude of the person dealing with the incident. All staff concerned with caring for pupils may contribute: the school secretary, support staff, meals supervisors and schoolkeeper all see a different facet of a pupil's behaviour. The wider the consensus, the less easy it becomes to blame a 'simple clash of personalities' for the problem.

## Incident report sheets

Negative incidents should be separately logged, indicating the date, time, place and name of the adult filing the report.

| Incident report no. | Date | |
|---|---|---|
| Time | Location | |
| Name | Form | Teacher |
| Supervising staff present | | |

What happened (liaison person's report)

Pupil's comment

Parent's comment

| Action agreed | File for reference | ☐ |
| | Contact liaison | ☐ |
| | Arrange meeting | ☐ |
| | Date of next meeting | |

## Map of problem area

As well as drawing up a plan of the school (see earlier), you may find it useful to outline features in the playground, or the seating area in the classroom, etc.

## Home–school meeting

This form is useful as a record of what is agreed at a home–school meeting.

| Date | Time |
|---|---|
| Location | Present |
| Agreed at meeting | |
| Decision | |
| Review date | Continue monitoring ☐ |

# Bullying in secondary schools

*Eric Jones*

## What this chapter will explore:

- Are anti-bullying strategies applicable to all secondary schools?
- Defining bullying
- Strategies to prevent bullying in secondary schools
- Dealing with excuses
- Steps to take when there is an incident
- Changing the ethos
- Professional concerns

There is a joke that occasionally does the rounds and which our profession finds amusing, even if it is a little cruel. The story is of a social worker, teacher or vicar (suit yourself) who comes across the bruised and battered victim of a mugging, stoops to look at the damage and exclaims, 'My goodness, I bet the person who did this has got some problems …!'

As professionals, we are as concerned as anyone with the underlying causes and reasons for the behaviour of the bully. We are interested in prevention, and so this chapter will outline some of the strategies already found useful in preventing outbreaks of bullying behaviour. We also have to act when a bullying incident has occurred, responding to both victim and culprit. We have to sanction, control and put strategies into place.

## Are anti-bullying strategies applicable to all secondary schools?

Bullying is always bad, but pupils in secondary school may find it harder to deal with than pupils in primary school. As one pupil said, 'I am older and understand things better so bullying hurts more now.' Bullies in secondary school are more experienced and clever at hiding what they are doing, or making better excuses when they are caught. Of course secondary pupils can also be very compassionate and get involved in schemes like peer support (see Chapter 11) to help stop bullying.

Strategies for dealing with bullying are applicable to any secondary school, regardless of its population. I am writing from my experiences in both an inner-city comprehensive (11+) and a private school. The inner-city school is surrounded by poor housing and unemployment, and there is considerable disenchantment on the part of many pupils and parents. Education, the law and the police are not looked upon with much enthusiasm.

Well over half the yearly intake arrives with a reading age two or more years behind their chronological age. Attracting teachers to fill vacancies and providing extra help for the seriously disadvantaged, academically or socially, is a logistical nightmare.

Nevertheless there is success. Many pupils achieve commendable examination results and some achieve outstanding success. Teachers are exhausted, yet justifiably pleased when an entire year group can go out on work experience, or when pupils in Year 7 pull up their reading age by over a year in the first few months.

There is also success in dealing with the problem of bullying. Interestingly, the same anti-bullying strategies have been effective in a middle-class, private boys' school south of London, where everyone can read well and nearly 100 per cent gain five or more A*–C grades at GCSE but where bullying still exists in various forms.

# Defining bullying

Is everything that gets labelled 'bullying' really that, or is it that because the victim says it is? Teachers should and do try to deal with problems, but not all problems may be bullying. The worry is that, quite often, teachers, parents and pupils talk about bullying when they ought to be talking about something else – rather in the same way that all headaches, to some people, come to be called migraines. That is not to say that there are no migraines, or that headaches are not serious in themselves. Everything needs to be dealt with for what it is. Consider the following behaviours.

## Mocking

None of us like pupils who mock and giggle, or point fingers at others for their idiosyncrasies. But these pupils are not 'career' bullies who pick out a weaker victim and repeatedly use strategies to make them feel small; they are pupils growing up and doing what pupils do, rather cruelly, but predictably. We must try to teach them better attitudes and solve the problems that they cause.

## Stealing

Nobody likes pupils who steal money or sweets from others, but beware of giving them the notoriety of being called bullies. They are thieves. We seek to teach them better social behaviour within the law. Bullies, in contrast, tend to extort money from a weaker victim or victims, systematically and repeatedly. This may be prompted by greed (and it is still theft) but primarily it is an act of power.

## Fighting

As teachers, we get remarkably fed up with pupils who scrap and fight with one another. But they are not bullies just because they fight, and the one who wins is most certainly not a bully because they win. You are not the victim of bullying because you come off worse! The mindless and degrading violence of the strong against the weak may be bullying, but fighting, by definition, is not.

## Growing up

There is a risk of offending people if I say that some so-called bullying is part of growing up and learning to cope. It does not excuse the bully, but some of the early and generally unacceptable behaviour of many pupils is predictable and may even be unavoidable. Until it actually becomes 'bullying' (premeditated and delib-erate) it may well just be part of growing up. As pupils move into their own circles and grow out of 24/7 adult supervision, many of them make the most dreadful mistakes in the way they treat each other. Perhaps it should be called the development of peer structures. They learn from it and before the rot of megalomania or dire timidity sets in, teachers should seek to direct the lessons they learn from it. Responsible adults must teach and guide. They must not allow unbridled nastiness and exploitation, but must allow pupils to grow and learn, from real situations, how to handle life itself. Both stronger and weaker pupils must be monitored.

## Unhealthy attention

Some pupils thrive on attention from older pupils. It can be healthy, but sometimes it is not. Young leaders can be a power of great good. The very best of prefectorial systems and uniformed youth organisations can vouch for this. Strong, greedy or mindless youngsters can also be a cancer in a young society. We often find that young victims, perhaps because they have no better example or model, and maybe even because they crave some attention, go back for more bullying, and are treated unmercifully, abused and exploited. It is a fact, however, that not all such peer structures and relationships are inevitably bad.

## Criminal insults and lies

Finally, within the meaning of bullying in the twenty-first century, we have to include emailing, social networking, setting up hate websites and text-messaging (see Chapter 4). Posting insults, photos and lies on the internet and electronically rubbishing your victim for all the world to read is a particularly insidious form of bullying. It is almost impossible for the victim to reverse once these things are online. This form of bullying stands alongside all the traditional methods and is equally unsociable and 'criminal'.

# Strategies to prevent bullying in secondary schools

## Talk about bullying

Talk about the possibilities of being bullied to your pupils even before they arrive at your school. On induction day (a day in the summer term when primary school pupils can come and spend a day at their new school), don't brush the subject aside. Bring it up, even if it does not arise naturally (as well it might) among the questions. During the first week in the new school, talk about bullying alongside information about where the toilets are, dinner queues or what happens if they are late. Let pupils know that sometimes there are bullies abroad, and that we do not tolerate them. Above all, do not try to pretend that there used to be bullies and now there are none. The trick is to establish a safe community in which you are 'allowed' and encouraged to report bullying, whether you are a victim or a friend of a victim.

## TOP TIP!

*When talking to parents, do not give the impression that, magically, 'Here in this school, bullies are a thing of the past.' It is better to mention the well-known fact that some pupils in every generation are nasty to others. Then you are free to inform parents about the attitudes of the school towards such pupils and their victims, strategies for prevention, how the school will respond, and so on. Make sure there is a school policy on bullying, print it and make it available (see Chapters 1 and 8).*

## Drama and tutorial work

If there is active tutorial work (and if not, why not?) use it to discuss bullying and prejudice. Mention bullying in assemblies. Use the perfect safety of drama lessons, or a dramatic piece in an assembly (created and composed by the youngsters themselves, of course), to show how to rebuff the bully's approach, or how to say 'No' to the thief, or how to 'go and tell'. Laugh at it, but be sure to prompt sensible discussion about what happens to the bully as well as the victim. Pupils can be very cruel towards the culprits (or alleged culprits) and perhaps they must face the ideas of forgiveness and responsibility to each other.

## Why not try this?

Use a game like this in assembly or in class to get your pupils talking:

One pupil plays the part of a manager or landlord, choosing who shall get the job or rent the flat. Or they could be a teacher choosing someone to be the form representative or a bus conductor deciding who in the queue can get on the bus which only has one available seat.

The authority figure then gives extreme and silly reasons why the applicant cannot be chosen. For example:

- 'I am sorry sir you cannot get on this bus. It is a woman's bus stop.'
- 'You cannot rent this flat because only people with green hair are allowed to live here.'
- 'You cannot have this job because you are wearing red trainers.'
- 'You cannot be form rep because only cabbages need apply.'

Use the discussion to explore the craziness of prejudices.

## Create a contract

It may be proper to tell pupils the school rules but it is even more important that they create their own, a contract, to refer to in their own group (see Chapter 13). This is a mutually agreed set of guidelines about what pupils (perhaps with your help) regard as good and bad, acceptable and unacceptable. Be sure to suggest that cyberbullying needs to be thought about, as pupils sometimes think that this is not 'real' bullying and is often outside the school anyway.

It can take a couple of sessions to create, edit and agree a contract, but in the end everyone signs it, including you, and it stays on the tutor group notice board. Of course it includes many things, maybe about the room, property, etc. In fact it takes a while to generate in detail but it ought to include the way we treat others, and what the school thinks of those who exploit and abuse others.

Here are a few examples of 'rules' created by 14-year-olds in my tutor group at the beginning of a new school year:

*We should respect each other equally ... and respect the hobbies, interests, skills and talents of others.*

*We should refrain from harmful insults and beware of jokes that can be hurtful. Insults are unnecessary ... to the face or indirectly.*

*We should never violate the rights of others ... we should allow each other space, to speak, to be involved or to be alone ...*

*We should always behave as if Mr Jones was in the room!*

*We can get by with a little help from our friends!*

### Why not try this?

As well as creating the contract for a new group thrown together as a class, why not celebrate everyone's individuality quite early on? This can be a process that takes weeks, or a few minutes at a time when available, but it is always rewarding.

From a simple, safe, questionnaire you can find out about pupils' interests, homework practices, modes of travel, hobbies, favourite TV, music, etc., and after sifting through all this information you make a 'State of the nation address'. It is all fairly light-hearted but all true. For example:

Nearly all of us watch *EastEnders* but nobody likes *Gardeners' World*, except the tutor! Nearly everyone spends at least two hours online. Only three come to school on foot and Jeremy has to take two buses and a train! Over 60 per cent of us do homework as soon as we get home, but nearly everyone admits to leaving some of it for late on Sunday evenings.

Having done this exercise, which is frankly good fun, and allowing a few weeks to get to know each other, continue with the theme. Everyone in the group writes a *positive comment* about everyone else: a simple statement acknowledging their particular skills or sense of humour. It can be an affectionate phrase, like 'He's a really good mate to have around' – and it is surprising just how honest and sensitive even 14+ year-old boys can be when asked to do this. You then collate and rewrite this without revealing named sources and eventually give every tutee an A4 sheet (or do it online) that outlines what their peers have said about them – and it is all positive.

I have found this exercise to have a dramatic effect on everyone's self-esteem and attitudes to others in the group. Just imagine receiving this as a true record of what your peers think of you:

> Almost everyone in the group mentions how friendly you are. Several thank you for your friendship, and even for helping them out (with homework!) sometimes. Your sense of humour matches plenty of others, so you can enjoy the same jokes, and most of the group think you are a good story-teller! They like it when you are on their team in.

## Avoid bullying by being there

Hopefully it is not too obvious to suggest that bullying might be avoided in some of its manifestations if the opportunities are not there for it to flourish. Teachers ought to be on time for lessons and be a presence in corridors, but we all know those who do not bother. It is easier to spend a little time being around than to spend a lot of time later sorting out what happened when the bullies stalked the quiet corners of the playground. (Worse still, somebody else has to sort it out!)

Beware the emergence of 'no-go areas'. 'Are you kidding?' said one colleague, 'I would never go round the back of there. You'd never come out alive!' That might be funny in the staffroom of a 1950s schoolboy story but it is not good enough in a modern school.

# Dealing with excuses

Some quick tests might help to take the wind out of the sails of bullies. Try these ideas to stop them in their tracks when they start to make excuses for their behaviour.

## 'It was only a joke'

One pupil who set up a website to harass another pupil claimed that she had done it for a laugh and that it was not really bullying. 'It was only a joke' is a phrase we all might have heard muttered at some time by the naughty pupil or hardened bully. The acid test is whether everyone is laughing. If they are not, then either it is not a joke or it is in very poor taste, and quite obviously directed against somebody. Tripping up, taking property, hitting, pushing into a corner, posting insults and nasty photos (often doctored to make the victim look ridiculous) online, and setting up hate websites are not jokes. If any person is the victim of the 'humour', then it is not a joke. Don't accept that as an excuse.

## 'We were only playing'

There it is again, and a very poor excuse it is for leaving somebody bruised and crying. The furious ball game is poor cover for knocking people over if the game was just that – a cover. If the person who gets knocked about was not playing (not part of the game) and, curiously, appears to be the same victim as yesterday, then it was not a game! Do not accept that it was. Incidentally, the reverse of this are the bullies who declare that they were playing, but in fact were joining in someone else's game unwanted and uninvited. Get the facts and put it to them that they were not playing, rather they were invading their game.

## 'It was an accident'

We have all heard this one. The victim ends up in a heap at the bottom of the stairs, or in a corridor, or with a torn bag and belongings scattered everywhere, but 'It was an accident'. This, too, has a foolproof test. If you did something accidentally to someone then you should stay behind and do what people normally do when they accidentally do such things . . . help! If you did not help the victim, apologise, assist, collect the belongings, take them to the nurse, etc., then it does not count as an accident, and we do not accept it as such. (Incidentally, the law does not allow you to drive on after a road traffic 'accident'. Not a bad lesson to learn.)

## 'I found it'

This is just one more cry from the bully who is in possession of someone else's property. If bullies and thieves knew how many times we have heard the 'I found it' excuse and how stupid it sounds, they would not use it. It is not acceptable. You will never convince the culprit that practically every person you have ever spoken to in similar circumstances used the same excuse. But you can ask the simple question, 'So, why did you keep it?'

## 'I was only borrowing'

That is a poor excuse for taking money or possessions from someone. Always ask, instantly, of the bully, 'Right then, what's his name? Where does he live? What class is he in? When's his birthday?' Anything, to prove that the bully knows nothing of the victim and had no way, and thus no intention, of returning the goods. You do not go around borrowing money from pupils you do not or barely know, and from weak anonymous little pupils. It is unacceptable, and if you do it, it very soon crosses the threshold from 'borrowing' into mugging. (I love telling such 'borrowers' that I can't wait for them to grow up and become bank managers, because, 'I'm going to come and borrow money from you and you won't even ask me where I live!')

## 'Do you accept there is a problem?'

The discussion with the alleged culprit might include the question, 'Do you accept there is a problem?' The chances are they will say 'Yes'. The allegations and the culprit's own written account (it is a good idea to ask for one), looked at calmly, will reveal that there is something to sort out. The discussion might go on to show that the victim had no choice as to the outcome: what happened, happened *to* the victim. But the alleged bully must face the fact that the situation could have been handled differently. The bully could have behaved differently and could have avoided being accused. The bully is responsible, because the bully was in control and *caused the problem*. We can say, 'You are responsible, and if you are a bully – so be it. We will deal with you. If you are not a bully, then apologise and learn. Accept that you made a mistake. Handle it differently next time and remember, all this is on record.'

> ### TOP TIP!
>
> *Do not allow the use of the words 'only' or 'just' when listening to or reading an account from somebody accused of bullying behaviour. These words are a cop-out: their own devaluation of the magnitude of the incident and a poor value judgement. If you do not believe that then try to explain your last car accident without using these words. Pupils must be encouraged to say 'I hit him' or 'I took the money', not 'I only hit him a bit' or 'I just took a few pence'. In a written account, cross out these two words. Nobody can be only a bit pregnant!*

# Steps to take when there is an incident

What pupils, parents and teachers *do* in the event of an incident will alter the dynamics of these situations. Indeed the first dynamic is that bullying will continue and thrive *unless* we do something about it. I call it the sad cycle, as illustrated in Figure 7.1.

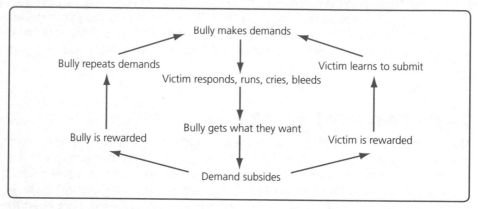

**Figure 7.1:** The sad cycle

So, how do we break this cycle?

## Telling

Pupils ought never succumb to the 'stay quiet or else' threat, whether spoken or implied. 'We did not say anything because it would have made it worse' is, frankly, crazy. Of course it is difficult for the victim, but *not* saying anything is worse, far worse. It means that a deliberate decision has been taken to allow the bullies to go on bullying as long as they like. We must help pupils to 'tell' and respond in such a way that they trust us.

Telling is crucial: not tomorrow, not when they get home, not a month later when the situation has become intolerable, but *now*. Of course, the advice about telling is fraught with danger. Some victims believe that the reward for telling is to be able to dictate the punishment – 'Is he going to be expelled, Miss?' Also, as a teacher you may be frantically busy most of the time, so you may need sometimes to qualify the 'tell now' instruction.

The best way is to have covered the dynamics of 'telling' during the discussions when pupils first arrive at the school, as already mentioned. Remember, too, that one push does not make a bullying; one hit does not make a beating. You want to know what is going on, but a brief record and a quick warning ought to be enough in the event of a single incident. Then, stay alert. The victim must be prepared to write an account of the incident, with help if need be, perhaps even overnight, and then let us deal with it.

## Instant retribution

Just because the pupil tells us immediately does not mean that there will be instant retribution. 'If it is revenge you want, you've come to the wrong place' is best said in the early days, well before incidents take place. On the strength of a reported incident you cannot drop everything and abandon a class, rushing off to mete out instant sanctions to the accused. However, then the victim invariably goes home and says, 'Miss So-and-so did nothing' and up comes mum, or dad, breathing fire. Just remember that not everything that is important, even urgent, is a crisis. A fire is a crisis. Bullying is important – so important that there should be no knee-jerk reaction.

If you confront the bully in a mood of crisis it will be a lost cause. 'Why did you hit so-and-so?' will almost certainly be rebuffed by, 'I didn't', or, worse, 'Who said I did?' to which you have no useful answer. The discussion is doomed. Bide your time. Similarly, if the victim is in distress, then you or another available teacher or staff member should deal with the distress or the injury. Deal with the bullying later. Don't rush in like a bull into the precarious china shop of negotiations.

## Written report

Ideally the best solution is to sit the pupil down and get a written report of the incident. That can be hours later, even days later, but of course the sooner the better. And there should be a similar record from the accused and any bystanders (written before they see each other). The problem is then taken on board, not in an air of crisis, but calmly. The written report is on record, which you can show the accused to warn them off. They can see the account. They ought to have written their own. If the bullying accusation has no foundation, they have nothing to fear. It will die a natural death and never be mentioned again. If it is the start of a 'career', then the facts *and* the warning are on record. If it is the most recent in a line of career incidents then of course you have a problem. So has the bully.

It is a good idea to use a simply designed 'incident report' (see Chapters 6 and 11) as a universal way of recording incidents in school. It needs a space for name, date, form, teacher, the incident and the action taken. Your computer software may already have this facility.

## Victim's diary

There is another form of written account that really does work. As teachers we are often confronted with the 'dripping tap' of bullying incidents – small, repeated, daily and usually silly incidents (perpetrated by different culprits, usually friends) which drive the victim to distraction but which, in themselves, are never very serious. Get the victim to keep a diary. For five or ten school days the pupil should not respond or overreact to these incidents but 'record' each one, noting the date, time, place, incident and who was the culprit. In the experience of more than one school the diary, when shown to those accused, has a startling effect. The 'chapter and verse' detail usually astounds them. For example, when you have called them in, line them up and calmly ask:

> Andrew, could you tell me why you kept taking chips off William's plate at lunch time last Thursday? It was his lunch, you know.

> Kevin, was there any reason for you throwing William's bag off the bus just as the doors were about to close? He had to get off and walk back for it.

> And Michael, William is getting a bit fed up with you calling him 'square head' every time you walk into the room. Would you be fed up if you heard that six times a day?

> And, please don't ask me how I know – it doesn't matter. He's doing GCSEs as well as you. He has to do homework, he has to come to school every day, and he's getting a bit fed up with you guys! Any ideas?

These pupils are not being told off or shouted at – not even sanctioned. They are simply being told that all their unacceptable behaviour is being monitored and that it is on record. It is almost like asking for their help! In 99 per cent of cases they apologise, say they had no idea that the victim was having such a regularly rotten time and agree to lay off. Of course, this also comes with a warning that that is precisely what you expect of them.

## Go public

Bullies hate knowing that you know what is going on and that the record is on file. They can see the facts if they wish. So can their family. Call their bluff. Go public. Tell the assembly what has been going on and what you have done about it. Mention no names, of course, but just make it perfectly clear that you do not tolerate bullying at this school, and why.

Sometimes this works in reverse. It is possible to announce in an assembly, 'I want to see, after this assembly, the people responsible for such-and-such an incident (but of course I won't mention your names here!).' After the assembly, up they come, never realising that you did not actually know who was going to appear. It is a tricky card to play, but when it works it's magic!

## Bring in the victims

This is controversial – and you or the victim's parents may not agree – but I think victims should not be kept at home 'until the incident is sorted out'. That is, unless it is extremely serious and there is reason to fear the victim might harm themselves if they are forced to come back to school. I feel you cannot sort out a one-sided account: the story your pupil has told you will not be the same story that you get from the accused. The accusations will be flying in all directions on the strength of a distraught phone call (the victim telling their mum on a mobile before they even mention it to a teacher, then going off home).

I have had situations in which the 'victim' – who actually made it all up to get out of PE – was sitting at home playing video games on their computer. It can be frustrating being stuck in the middle, bursting blood vessels and accusing people with no real evidence; while mum is fuming at 'that dreadful school', the alleged culprit is indignant, and the 'victim' is dipping their hand into their second packet of crisps. Mum has to bring the victim in, or send them in, and make some contribution to the solution. Most accusations of bullying are not made up, but it does happen.

The parents of the accused need to be invited as well. Again, not in an air of crisis, but calmly. Say to parents: 'There is something you ought to know, if possible today. Can you come and pick him up from school? I'll keep him until you get here.' Or: ' We have a problem and I'd like you to be here, perhaps to help sort it out. Your daughter could be excluded, but first can you come and see me straight away, like tomorrow morning?' Put the onus on parents to come and have some control over their pupil's destiny. Children are their parents' responsibility – not, in the end, ours.

If you can bring the victim and bully into the school, you may have a chance to deal with the problem before it gets completely out of hand.

---

### Case study

Robert was doing GCSEs. Slightly overweight, eager to do well, not keen on sport, keeping himself to himself, he was an easy target but not the victim of any particular bully. There was no major attack, no actual violence, nothing overtly aggressive from any individual or group.

However, there was a continuous tapping into his daily life with minute annoyances, which were wearing him down. This was low-level bullying. Reporting any one incident would have seemed petty, but the constant repetitive acts by uncaring pupils were driving him up the wall. When his tutor noticed it, Robert was willing to talk chapter and verse. But  ➡

he never thought that a solution could be found. He just wanted to keep his head down and not make a fuss.

His tutor asked him to keep a diary. 'Write down everything for a fortnight,' he was told. 'When, where, what and who.'

Two weeks later the tutor brought in everyone whose name had been mentioned in the diary. The pupils were puzzled and asked one another what they had in common. The tutor started outlining each incident with details, and asked 'Why?' The bag kick, the silly name-tags, pushing books off a desk, pinching things off his plate at lunch, chalk on his jacket – none of them major but cumulatively creating a miserable existence. 'How about some grown-up empathy with Robert?' the tutor asked. 'He's doing exams like you, he has work to do, and he has a right to do it without fending you off 10 times a day.'

The outcome was astonishing. 'It was a joke,' was the common response. 'We didn't know it really bothered him.' 'He must be fed up to the teeth.' The incidents stopped. Most of the pupils apologised. All understood that Robert did not deserve such treatment and, importantly, that it was now on the record. There were no sanctions, no telling off, no retribution; just putting it all behind them and moving on, learning a lesson and growing up. And even if one culprit had felt aggrieved that he had been reported, recorded and spoken to – tough! That's life.

Had the incidents been more vicious, with the bullies in an organised group and making Robert feel threatened, it would have been wise to bring the culprits in one by one and break their collective power (see Chapter 13). But the pupils bothering Robert were just a loose group feeding off each other.

## Exclusion

If you have a serious, unrepentant, bully who is a danger to other pupils, exclusion may be the sanction decided upon. In that case, yet again, be sure to report reasons and everyone's account. Play it by the book, and insist upon a proper interview with parents before readmission. Our concern as teachers is to build a relationship between aggressor, family and school, not just to mete out sanctions. We are not in the 'eye for an eye' business. The victim should not see the outcome as some kind of victory over the culprit. All concerned should try to achieve an outcome in which victims feel they have been supported, need fear no more, and in which the bully and their family feel the school has dealt with the situation compassionately, if strictly, for the benefit of all. The culprit is welcomed back, having 'served their time'. Such outcomes are rarely perfect, but are achievable and should be the objective.

## Cyberbullying

Chapter 4 covers this in detail, but it is worth emphasising that in secondary schools mobile phones and computers are here to stay. There were times when everyone was up in arms about having ballpoint pens in school, even watches – and calculators! Heaven forbid. But today we must accommodate all the wonderful technology, even though it makes bullying that much more difficult to deal with in school. Some schools have banned mobiles on campus (even though they can be very useful when trying to find a pupil at lunch time!). But even if phones are allowed, using the internet and cyberspace to bully and ridicule others, for all the world to see, can never be tolerated. Stamp on it. I get so angry about it, I might even stamp on the phone.

Cyberbullying is insidious, cruel and totally unacceptable. The photograph, the cartoon, the untrue statement, the 'joke' to which the victim has no reply – such behaviour beggars belief. So, as a general rule and as advice to victims, I advise them:

● do not answer

● do not reply

● do not erase.

And try not to let it phase you. Ignore it!

With a bit of luck, and with some help from the police or service provider, it is possible to track down the perpetrator. Even if it is not, then as soon as it becomes known that the school has 'involved' the police, you will be amazed how quickly cyberbullying dries up.

## Involving the law

We should not fear to teach or remind bullies about common law. The laws concerning assault, threatening behaviour, actual bodily harm and theft apply to them as much as to every other citizen. You can advise victims' families that they have the option to go to the law, and offer to cooperate if they do. If, however, they ask the school to deal with an incident, as invariably they do, then make two things clear to all concerned:

● To the victim and family: having asked the school to deal with it, they must let the school get on with it.

- To the accused and family: they must cooperate with the authority of the school because the victim's family has asked the school to handle things instead of going to the police.

See www.childrenslegalcentre.com for current laws regarding bullying – or why not ask your pupils to do this as an assignment to enlighten them?

## Changing the ethos

We all know that bullying in various forms exists in schools (and other institutions) and that we should try to prevent it and respond to it in a positive way, with an outcome that hopefully benefits all. We want the school to be a better place – for likely victims, likely bullies, and all others who work and play there. If a school declares that their policy and their strategies are helpful and tend to work, in an ongoing lively community, then we applaud them. If a school tries to convince us that the problem is solved and that there is no more bullying, then we tend not to believe them.

Schools are ongoing, living and changing communities. You never solve anything once and for all. Each new intake of pupils has to learn how to behave, as 11, 13, 15-year-olds. But it should be possible to create an atmosphere in school in which maltreatment of one's peers is not acceptable and is openly discussed – an atmosphere in which incidents are reported, recorded and dealt with. A policy that is understood and followed.

I have visited, by invitation, several schools once a year for several years, presenting a two-hour session which helps set the tone for teachers and tutors to build on as the term proceeds. My input is minimal, but hopefully helpful, and pupils will nearly always listen to an outside voice. Those schools, however, do report that over six or seven years (with continual work) the entire ethos changes. Slowly, imperceptibly, bullying does become a thing of the past – a different phenomenon approached head-on and dealt with. The entire school absorbs the policy and adopts the 'we don't tolerate it here' philosophy.

Perhaps this is a good moment to refer back to the proactive strategies shown earlier. Early discussion of the possibility of bullying, and a mutually agreed contract created in a positive atmosphere, *could* lead directly to very few incidents occurring. At the other extreme, with little or no action, or a timid approach, a bully might return again and again to their unacceptable behaviour, provoking incidents.

In the inner city there are youngsters suffering from startling disadvantages. Those with stunted growth, bad burns scars, disabilities, as well as non-English speaking refugees, all may become victims of the strong mindless bully, alongside the weak, the clever, the creative and the bookworm. The suggestion is, however, that defining an anti-bullying policy, encouraging discussion and dealing firmly with the potential and the actuality of bullying do help to create an atmosphere in which youngsters learn that bullying does not pay.

You will never see all the bullying that goes on. But it is important to continue to keep proper records of even minor incidents, then forgive and promote the relationships involved. You will want to make it worthwhile for pupils to trust and involve you, so that you can solve what is possible, report and refer elsewhere what isn't, and never fear to admit that pupils are sometimes nasty to each other.

## TOP TIP!

*'Run along and stop making a fuss' is not helpful when a pupil reports something. The chances are that they have not reported up to that point, and that 'telling' comes when they can take no more. It is a brave and scary decision. To be dismissed by a 'busy' teacher could tip them over the edge. So, always listen and be there when you are needed.*

## Professional concerns

I began this chapter by describing a teaching situation in an inner-city context. I conclude by putting the teacher and the bully into a teaching perspective. The teacher's professional concern is with the bully and their victim, as pupils. But, with the best will in the world, it cannot be the teacher's total preoccupation. The wonder is not that teachers deal quite successfully with some bullying, but that they have time to handle any of it at all!

The whole business of negotiating and consulting (with pupils, among ourselves, with the local authority and with parents) occupies thousands of hours of meetings. What that does to the general atmosphere of schools and learning can only be guessed at. Having 'supply' or 'cover' teachers, sometimes several times a day, is not good for pupils, for discipline, or for the continuity of courses.

Secondary school teachers may well be in contact with 400+ different pupils a week. A 60–70 hour week is not uncommon, much of it spent in exasperating negotiations, meetings and continual justification of actions. The mental exhaustion has to be experienced to be understood.

A lot of discussion has taken place in recent times about methods of teaching. Teachers, as always, have been caught in the middle of 'experts' vying with one another for sound-bite headlines about what's best for our pupils in our schools, and what teachers need to do today, tomorrow or the day after. Perhaps the gradual abolition of 'battery-taught' pupils – in rows, with narrow discipline and curriculum methods (unsatisfactory though that was in many ways) – might just have left little room for 'free-range bullies'.

## Conclusion

Everyone has the right to go home happy at the end of the day (and with the same number of teeth and amount of property they arrived with!), be they pupils or teachers. Our task is to see that, as far as possible, it always happens. Even the culprit and their family have the right to go home feeling they have been fairly treated. We have to open up the field for discussion and put bullying on the agenda of the school – building relationships in an open and learning atmosphere in which bullying is unacceptable.

I usually end my school presentations with this summary:

- Bullies, remember:
  - This school does not tolerate bullying.
  - Bullying is unacceptable.
  - You do not have to be a bully.
  - Victims have a right and a duty to *tell*.
  - You may have to learn to apologise.

- Victims, remember:
  - This school does not tolerate bullying.
  - Bullying is unacceptable.
  - You do not have to be bullied.
  - You have a right and a duty to *tell*.
  - You may have to learn to forgive.

- Bystanders, remember:
  - This school does not tolerate bullying.
  - Bullying is unacceptable.
  - You have an obligation and a duty to report bullying and tell the truth about what you see.
  - Bullying is not an observer sport unless you wish to be associated with the offence.

And how do I start my presentations? A few years ago I spoke to the teachers at a small school in Croydon, and, returning to speak to the governors a few weeks later, found the following notice on the wall. I removed it, copied it, sought permission from the 8-year-old writer and even paid him a royalty! He could be married with several children by now, but when he was 8, he wrote this:

*Bullies are cruel and nasty.*
*They hurt your feelings or hurt you physically*
*And start to destroy your happiness.*
*They even make you do things you do not want to do.*
*People don't like bullies,*
*They're rude, nasty and mean.*
*I don't like bullies – nor does anyone else!*

*Have you ever been bullied? (Yes!)*
*Have you been made to cry? (Yes!)*
*Or been made to feel small and useless,*
*Just nothing, just a nobody?*
*Yes, that happened to me.*
*Tell your mum or a teacher,*
*Dinner lady or headteacher about the bullying.*
*Tell them who it is, then it may stop.*

The astonishing thing about this piece of doggerel is its insight. The 8-year-old knows things that all victims know and that all teachers should remember. Bullies make you *feel bad* (above hurting you physically). It's making someone feel bad and useless that is the real crime of the bully.

And this little poet also hits the solution on the head. *Tell* somebody. The bully's greatest weapon is their anonymity – the thing the bully relies upon most. So burst that particular bubble and you are well on the way to prevention and solution. Make telling legitimate.

And even then, our little poet only suggests that it *may* stop. He's realistic enough to know that there is no certain answer, and that even in poetry nobody can promise that it *will* stop!

The continuing, and hopefully rewarding, task of all of us must be to anticipate, prepare, prevent and respond to bullying if it arises. Then we must take whatever time is needed to put the situation right. Teachers continue to strive to do just that.

## Going further

### Useful websites

www.childrenslegalcentre.com

www.ericjones.co.uk

# Helping victims
## *Andrew Mellor*

### What this chapter will explore:

- Bullying is not the victim's fault
- Avoiding labels
- Belief in change
- The anguish of victims
- Can the law protect victims?
- Creating an effective anti-bullying policy
- Giving victims a voice
- Cyberbullying
- Victims and teachers working together

Bullying cannot be cured just by treating the victims. They are not suffering from a disease but are involved in complex social situations, each one unique and requiring individual action. Parents, teachers, friends and bystanders all play a part in the confrontation between bully and victim, so they must also be included in any coping strategy.

Parents or teachers working alone have little chance of successfully helping victims unless a school has a clear, well-developed anti-bullying policy. Many schools do, but some have only a scrap of paper that lists unrealistic claims and unkept promises. The first step towards an effective anti-bullying policy must be to create a climate of concern: members of the school community, adults and pupils, must understand the feeling of helplessness experienced by victims.

## Bullying is not the victim's fault

*I think I felt that I was the only person that had ever been bullied and if I told anybody they would think I was stupid and a wimp.*

(11-year-old girl)

Victims need to be reassured that they are not alone and that it could happen to anyone; all it takes is to be in the wrong place at the wrong time. Such an assertion may contradict the popular wisdom of the playground:

*I would say that bullying usually happens to people who are different (for example, their colour, religion or some disability). People who are shy or have a weak character are usually the ones who are bullied.*

(15-year-old girl)

If this is believed by victims then they may feel, however erroneously, that they are to blame for what has happened. The endless repetition of bullying taunts can cause so much distress that rational thought becomes impossible. Pupils may believe that they are being bullied because they are fat, wear spectacles, are shy or just different, and that no one, least of all an adult, can help. It only takes one bad experience to confirm this belief:

*When a friend told the teacher I was being bullied, he said I was old enough to deal with it myself.*

(14-year-old girl)

With increased awareness of the damage that bullying can do, it might reasonably be thought that such a response from an adult is much less likely than it once was. However, if one hard-pressed, overworked teacher makes an honest but mistaken judgement about the seriousness of a complaint, that can mean that the opportunity is lost for adults to intervene in a potentially damaging bullying episode.

A firm and clear discipline policy will never succeed in tackling bullying unless strategies are adopted that encourage victims to seek adult help. The taboo against telling that exists in British society ensures that pupils will go through agonies before seeking help. It is not only the threat of physical retaliation that deters them but also the endlessly repeated playground taunts:

*Tell-tale tit, your mammy cannae knit.*

*Your daddy cannae go to bed without a dummy-tit.*

(Scottish playground rhyme)

Schools must create an atmosphere in which telling is always encouraged and teachers must create situations in which telling is possible. But this still leaves the victim with the responsibility of judging if an incident should be reported or shrugged off. Will the complaint be treated seriously and wisely?

*I honestly don't know if I would tell someone if I was being bullied. I would feel I was being silly about the whole thing. I'd be too frightened in case I'd be laughed at.*

(15-year-old girl)

Most older pupils will have learned through experience to assess the gravity of bullying and identify those incidents that are likely to be taken seriously – and which adults are best to approach. However, younger pupils do not have this experience to draw on. Anything that is happening to them at the time is serious and, for all they know, permanent. Teachers of such pupils run the risk of being overwhelmed by trivia, so it is perhaps understandable that they may on occasion seem less than welcoming.

# Avoiding labels

Although the words 'bully' and 'victim' are used to describe pupils who bully and those who are bullied, it is important that you do not use these words in discussion with pupils when sorting out bullying. It has nothing to do with political correctness and everything to do with not making things worse than they already are.

A pupil who experiences bullying in one setting will often come to believe that it will happen elsewhere.

## Case study

A 12-year-old girl was bullied so badly in one school that her parents moved her to another. Naturally she was anxious that the same thing might happen in her new school. And that is exactly what happened. Her anxiety made it difficult for her to make new friends and made her vulnerable to bullying once more. Well-meaning adults had acknowledged that she  ➡

was an innocent victim of bullying and had encouraged her to try to change her behaviour; they said that she should not let the bullying pupils see that she was upset by their actions. She tried to do this but failed. So she came to believe that, because of her own weakness, she had brought it all upon herself and would continue to be bullied.

If adults wish to counter such a self-fulfilling prophecy they must never say to distressed pupils that they are 'victims'. Doing so merely increases the chances that the pupils will continue to be just that.

Neither, however provoked they are, should they call a particular pupil a 'bully'. It is one thing to say, 'That is bullying and it is bad and you should not do it', and quite another thing to say, 'You are a bully' or, even worse, 'You are a bad little bully.' After all, if a young boy is not doing very well at school and the only thing that he is good at and that gives him any feeling of power is making others miserable, then being awarded the tag of 'bully' might give him a status among his peers that he cannot achieve any other way.

## Belief in change

We have moved away from the idea that bullying is just an inevitable part of growing up but we have some way to go before we can be confident that we can tackle all incidents of bullying effectively. Schools can work towards achieving that aim but, to do so, all members of a school community must share some fundamental beliefs. They should be able to say, with real conviction:

*We believe that all forms of bullying, whatever the age or position of the people involved, are wrong.*

*We believe that nobody ever deserves to be bullied.*

*We believe that people who bully others must accept the consequences of their actions.*

And, most importantly:

*We believe in the possibility of redemption: people who bully others can change.*

Without that last belief the only logical response to school bullies would be to expel them. Since research consistently shows that 40 per cent or more of people surveyed admit to having bullied others at some time, such a strategy would leave most school rolls rather depleted.

# The anguish of victims

Research shows that being a victim of school bullying is a common experience, but it is the words of pupils rather than statistics that reveal the anguish of victims – and how adults often underestimate the scale and seriousness of a problem:

> *I am scared stiff all the time and my schoolwork is being affected. I am also scared to go out. I want to stand up to the girl who is bullying me because she is making my life a misery, but I can't.*
>
> (14-year-old girl)

As pupils grow up, they appear to be less likely to become victims, presumably because they develop protective or avoidance strategies of their own. But older girls seem to do this better than older boys, who sometimes feel that they have no one to turn to:

> *I have been picked on. People think I am nothing and say anything they want to me. Every day I feel rejected. It's not that people use violence much but I feel as if I am treated as a dustbin. I do want to come forward about this but as I am leaving in a few months I don't see any reason to do so. Nor have I the courage.*
>
> (16-year-old boy)

Few older teenage boys will admit to being the victims of bullying, but those that do can feel a sense of alienation, failure and despair:

> *Sometimes you feel like dying because you can't face up to it.*
>
> (15-year-old boy)

When it comes to dealing with bullying, boys often suggest that victims should stand up for themselves. Girls, on the other hand, are more likely to accept that the answer to bullying lies in the adoption of a collective remedy:

> *People that are being bullied feel as if they are alone in that problem and that most people, if not everybody, are against them. They need to be shown that they are not alone and that unless they tell somebody, nothing can be done.*
>
> (15-year-old girl)

There is a particular problem around bullying and young men. Many societies, including our own, send messages that young men should be tough but, paradoxically, punish those who fight and alienate those who reject violence. No wonder adolescent boys are sometimes mixed up. They are encouraged to stick up for themselves, although they are not given clear guidance as to what is an appropriate level of force (if any) to use if they are attacked. In school they are told by adults that those who use violence are bad but among their peers they often find that being tough and willing to use force can give social status.

An older boy who is not aggressive and who is bullied by others may lose so much status that life becomes unbearable. Seeking help could be perceived as a further sign of weakness. Older girls are much readier to seek help. It is clear that schools must try to develop an ethos in which nobody, of whatever age or whatever sex, must ever feel that there is any shame in speaking openly about fears or concerns.

# Can the law protect victims?

Pupils have the right to be educated in an atmosphere that is free from fear. Headteachers and others responsible for running schools have a duty to do all that they reasonably can to protect pupils in their charge from intimidation, assault or harassment. This right and this duty are enshrined within documents such as the UN Convention on the Rights of the Child, the Pupils (Scotland) Act 1995 and the European Convention on Human Rights.

Schools are also subject to the law of the land. Assault, harassment and intimidation are offences, whatever the age of the perpetrator or victim. Despite this, teachers are often reluctant to refer incidents to the police. Sometimes there may be good reasons for not involving the police but at other times it seems that an assault against a pupil is treated less seriously than if the victim were an adult.

The Human Rights Act allows people to claim their rights under the European Convention on Human Rights. Although the Act does not contain any specific mention of the right of a pupil to be protected from bullying, it may make it more likely that authority and school policies and practices will be challenged in the courts. The threat of litigation looms ever larger in the minds of school managers.

In recent years a number of victims or their parents have taken legal action against schools, alleging that not enough has been done to protect them from bullying. The Anti-Bullying Network has published an information sheet on its website (www.antibullying.net) which discusses the pros and cons of involving a solicitor.

The possible advantages of taking legal action include the following:

- Victims and their families sometimes feel that their concerns are not being treated seriously. Involving a solicitor can change this.
- A solicitor can provide support to individuals who may feel powerless against school authorities.
- A court decision in favour of a victim could help that person come to terms with their experiences by ruling that the school did not act properly.
- The court may order that damages be paid as compensation for the harm suffered.
- A high-profile court case can help to clarify the duty of schools to protect victims. This could make it less likely that others will suffer in the future.

Possible disadvantages of taking legal action include the following:

- It can be very stressful. If the case is defended, an emotionally fragile victim may be subjected to lengthy cross-examination.

- Any resolution will be severely delayed. Papers have to be prepared and witnesses who are willing to testify must be found. Meanwhile victims and their families will not be able to put the events behind them and get on with the rest of their lives. A Scottish girl took her local council to court over school bullying. It was 10 years before the case was heard, by which time she was in her mid-twenties.

- The outcome is uncertain. The girl mentioned above lost.

- Enormous expense can be involved, especially if the claimant does not receive legal aid. A Derby girl lost her case and was ordered to pay the council's costs, which were estimated at £30,000. The judge in that case revealed that even if she had won she would only have been awarded £1,250.

- Once a headteacher knows that there is a possibility of legal action, it will become more difficult for them to admit that mistakes may have been made and that a new approach is needed.

The law certainly has a place in defining what protection should be given to actual and potential victims of bullying. It also provides a means of redress when things go wrong. However, as it operates at the moment, the legal system is slow, expensive and cumbersome. The onus is on the victim to prove fault. Local authorities and their insurers fight every case vigorously for fear of conceding expensive precedents. Victims with limited emotional and financial resources face an unequal battle, which has the potential to cause them as much harm as the original bullying.

# Creating an effective anti-bullying policy

Bullying happens in every school in the country, although research suggests that some experience more than others. Attempts to explain these differences in terms of geography, social class, family background, deprivation or privilege are not convincing.

Schools must now have anti-bullying policies (see Chapter 13). Observing schools that are tackling bullying effectively leads me to believe that whatever the moral, religious or disciplinary standards of a school, there are three prerequisites for the creation of a successful anti-bullying policy:

- **Honesty** – Teachers and parents must be prepared to acknowledge that a problem might exist. Headteachers have a right to expect support from parents and the community if they admit that a problem exists and take positive steps to address it.

● **Openness** – The creation of an open atmosphere is a major challenge to schools. It has consequences that go beyond making it easier for victims of bullying to speak out: pupils will talk about other problems, at home or elsewhere; they will be more likely to challenge school rules that they perceive to be unfair; and they will make more complaints against teachers.

● **Involvement** – If parents, teachers and pupils are all involved in formulating an anti-bullying policy they will have a vested interest in making sure it succeeds.

Just how these ideals are to be achieved will vary from school to school. To be effective, any policy must recognise the history and traditions of the school; it must build on existing strengths and repair recognised weaknesses. This could be achieved in stages:

| Stage | Groups involved |
|---|---|
| 1  Recognition | Teachers and parents |
| 2  Investigation | Teachers and pupils, possibly with outside help |
| 3  Consultation | Teachers, parents, pupils and ancillary staff |
| 4  Implementation | As above |
| 5  Evaluation and modification | Teachers using existing consultation procedures |

## Stage 1 – recognition

In the past, individual parents who have complained about bullying have felt isolated. They were often told that their child's problems were exceptional incidents, or they were told that there was nothing that the school could do. A report showing that there was little or no bullying could easily be concocted by a headteacher who was determined to sweep things under the carpet.

It is possible that the schools that have already developed anti-bullying policies are those where headteachers and staff are most progressive and receptive to the notion that education is about more than just academic endeavour. If this is true, then campaigners for change in the remaining schools will have a particularly difficult task. A very powerful argument they can use is that all schools in the UK are now officially encouraged to develop anti-bullying policies. Schools that fail to do this, or which do it in a tokenistic way, risk censure by school inspectors. More importantly, these schools give out the message that bullying does not matter.

## Stage 2 – investigation

Teachers are in the best position to carry out this process, working with pupils. Guidance teachers or those responsible for pastoral care have the opportunity to carry out surveys as part of a programme of social education. In other schools it could be teachers of religious education, social subjects or English who do the work. This process can also involve teachers who would not normally see the reduction of bullying as being part of their role. For example, teachers with mathematical or computing skills can undertake the analysis of questionnaire surveys. The result of the surveys will allow an assessment of the size of the problem and should also indicate any aspect that needs special attention, such as particular age groups or places where bullying is common. Sometimes, such a survey will reveal other, related problems and highlight how specific policies in areas such as pupil protection, anti-racism or equal opportunities may need to be examined and modified.

## Stage 3 – consultation

A successful strategy to defeat bullying needs the cooperation of teachers, parents, pupils and anyone else involved with a school. Schools with a consensus style of management will be best able to do this. However, authoritarian headteachers may feel threatened by this suggestion, so the degree of involvement will vary widely between schools. In Norway, where extensive work on preventing bullying has been pioneered, special meetings about bullying are held, to which parents, pupils and teachers are invited. Pupils sit with their parents, rather than as a group, and all are invited to contribute to the discussion. A DVD may be shown first to create the right climate, and the parents may be given the result of a school survey on bullying.

An alternative to an open meeting specifically about bullying is to raise the topic at a meeting of the parent teacher association. The disadvantage of this is that it could exclude pupils from the discussion. No policy against bullying can be successful without their active cooperation.

An increasing number of Scottish schools have school (or pupil) councils. However, it is difficult to know how many of those that do exist are functioning well or are merely tokenistic. At their best, school councils are a way of encouraging the active participation of pupils in shaping and reviewing the school's behaviour policy in order to foster a sense of collective commitment to it.

## Why not try this?

Even if you do not have a pupils' council, it is surely necessary to have some mechanism for consultation. The sheer size of most secondary schools means that it is not practicable to have a council composed of all pupils and teachers. An alternative is to have an elected body, with each year group choosing one or two representatives. But this has the disadvantage that the representatives may become distanced from their electorate, especially if their efforts seem to produce little effect. Schools that totally reject the idea of pupil councils could utilise the guidance or year group system to measure opinion, with teachers holding discussions within tutor groups and reporting back to management. In this system pupils would have no direct voice and would not be responsible for the agenda, so such a system might be more acceptable in a school with a traditional, authoritarian ethos.

## Stages 4 and 5 – implementation, evaluation and modification

These stages, together with the previous one, form an interlinked and continuing process. Whatever policy a school adopts, regular consultation must continue. Without this there is a danger that the bullying policy will become just another booklet filed away until the next visit from the school inspectors.

## Protection and support for victims

It is likely that you will discover various bullying flashpoints during the consultation process. Perhaps it is common on school buses or in the playground. Maybe it happens at certain times of the day, for example during the morning interval. Playgrounds are often unsupervised and victims may have literally nowhere to hide. Sometimes bullying involves only a small group of pupils while others are only vulnerable at particular times, perhaps during a family crisis or after transfer from another school. Sometimes bullying is found to be happening in classrooms, which can be a challenging fact for teachers to accept.

In all these cases supervision arrangements will have to be carefully reviewed. It is not enough to tell pupils that they will be safe if they spend their break and lunch times in sight of the staffroom windows. This merely adds to the victim's sense of isolation and may increase their attractiveness as a target for the bullies. Supervision must be carried out by a teacher who has been trained to spot signs of bullying and can provide appropriate support for victims.

Of course pupils cannot be supervised all the time – to do so would restrict their freedom to develop as individuals – but they can be protected in situations where bullying is known to be common. Pupils themselves can help to provide this protection, but they will need the assurance that any sanctions to be imposed are sufficiently strong to deter retribution against a helpful bystander.

Counselling and support should be provided for victims who have been seriously affected by their experiences. This could come from a guidance teacher, educational psychologist, or simply a trained adult with whom the pupil can identify. But pupils will only seek such assistance if bullying has been raised as a topic during normal classwork. This can happen in social education, English, drama or RE – it does not really matter where, providing it is dealt with seriously and it is unequivocally condemned.

Of course, support for victims will not serve much purpose unless the people doing the bullying are helped to modify their behaviour in some way. Indeed, if support for victims is the only remedy on offer it can send out the unintended but hurtful message that they are at fault because they are the ones that have to change (see Chapter 9 about helping bullies). This is the lie that bullies tell their victims. It is a lie they believe, and this belief can have serious long-term consequences.

# Giving victims a voice

Victims of bullying should always be involved in any discussions about possible remedies. We should encourage pupils to *talk* rather than *tell* when they are being bullied, as a sign that this will be a two-way process in which their opinions and their fears will be fully respected.

Pupils who are being bullied often say that the main reason they have not told an adult is that they fear that the adult, however well meaning, will do something to make the bullying worse. As a minimum, pupils should always be told about any action that is being taken on their behalf. It is much better, however, if time is taken to discuss and agree any proposed action with them.

Pupils who have experienced bullying will have opinions about their school's policy on bullying as well as about how their own particular experiences were handled. They could have a key role in helping to improve anti-bullying strategies – if they are encouraged to speak out, and if schools set up mechanisms designed to facilitate this.

The UN Convention on the Rights of the Child states that a child:

> who is capable of forming his or her own views [has] the right to express those views freely in all matters affecting the child, the views of the child being given due weight in accordance with the age and maturity of the child.

The Standards in Scotland's Schools etc. (Scotland) Act 2000 charges headteachers with a specific duty to consult pupils:

*The development plan shall include an account of the ways in which, and extent to which, the headteacher of the school will consult the pupils in attendance at the school; and seek to involve them, when decisions require to be made concerning the everyday running of the school.*

The full implications of this legal requirement to consult pupils are as yet unclear, but it would be very difficult to defend a headteacher who wrote a school anti-bullying policy without any meaningful input from pupils, especially those who have first-hand experience to inform their views.

## Why not try this?

You can help pupils who have given input after being bullied, or who have told you about the bullying, by:

- praising them for telling;
- reassuring them that the bullying will be stopped;
- giving them time to talk about their feelings;
- identifying a subject or activity the pupil enjoys and encourage them to shine;
- giving them extra responsibility, like being 'pilots' who show new pupils around the school;
- appointing them as a classroom monitor – tidying desks, handing out books, etc.;
- asking them to help younger children with their reading;
- involving them in activities like gym or art exhibitions;
- suggesting they think about getting involved in activities outside school like martial arts, music or drama;
- giving them opportunities to draw or write about feelings, perhaps in a diary.

If the victims are fortunate enough to have counselling, you can also work with the counsellor to ensure you are complementing their efforts.

# Cyberbullying

Cyberbullying (see Chapter 4) makes it ever more difficult for adults to protect vulnerable pupils. But we should never forget that technology is morally neutral and can be a channel for comfort as well as threats. The phone line that carries a threatening text message may also carry information and advice to an anxious parent or a worried pupil. While technology can be used to bully, the internet can also be a sanctuary for the victims of bullying by masking their alleged 'differences' and allowing them to be part of communities beyond their local one.

No doubt even more new ways of one person being nasty to another are being developed as you read this. For example, there have been reports of school reunion sites being used to slander ex-pupils and teachers alike. A Scottish secondary school had to take its chatroom offline due to aggressive bullying activity. A phenomenon called 'bluejacking' (sending anonymous text messages over short distances using Bluetooth wireless technology) has also been reported.

Although cyberbullying may be taking advantage of cutting-edge technology, the motives of those who are doing this and the excuses they make for their behaviour are age-old. Cyberbullying is different from 'ordinary' bullying because:

- Technology allows the user to bully anonymously or from an unknown location.
- No place, not even a bedroom, provides sanctuary from the intrusion of a threatening text message or an abusive email.
- Cyberbullying leaves no physical scars so it is, perhaps, less evident to a parent or teacher, but it is highly intrusive and the hurt it causes can be very severe.
- Young people are particularly adept at adapting to new technology, an area that can often seem a closed world to adults. For example, the numerous acronyms used by young people in chatrooms and in text messages (POS – parents over shoulder, TUL – tell you later) make it difficult for adults to recognise potential threats.

To prevent cyberbullying in your school, you need to:

- Find out about any relevant guidelines that are published by your local authority or governing body.
- Be prepared to close down any website or chatroom under your control if it is used to send bullying or threatening messages.
- Agree a code of conduct. If the particular service is used by a relatively small number of pupils, any discussion could involve all users. If the service involves large numbers of pupils, a representative group should be assembled and tasked with agreeing a code. All users should be required to agree to abide by this code.
- Make sure that pupils who use messaging, email, mobile or web services know that any messages they send or post may be read by an adult.
- Make sure that pupils know that sending abusive or threatening messages is against the law.

## Why not try this?

Here are some points that could be included in the anti-cyberbullying code of conduct that teachers could discuss and agree with pupils. Use these points to help start the discussion, but aim to end up with a small number (up to five or so) of short statements that are suitable for the age of the users.

- If you feel you are being bullied by email, text or online, do talk to someone you trust.

- Never send any bullying or threatening messages. Anything you write and send could be read by an adult.

- Serious bullying should be reported to the police – for example, threats of a physical or sexual nature.

- Keep and save any bullying emails, text messages or images.

- If you can, make a note of the time and date when bullying messages or images were sent, and note any details about the sender.

- Try logging into a chatroom with a different user ID or nickname. That way the bully will not know who you are. You could change your mobile phone number and only give it out to close friends.

- Contact the service provider to tell them about the bullying. They may be able to track the bully down.

- Use blocking software – you can block instant messages from certain people or use mail filters to block emails from specific email addresses.

- Don't reply to bullying or threatening text messages or emails – this could make matters worse. It also lets the bullying people know that they have found a 'live' phone number or email address. They may get bored quite quickly if you ignore them.

- Don't give out your personal details online – if you are in a chatroom, watch what you say about where you live, the school you go to, your email address, etc. All these things can help someone who wants to harm you to build up a picture about you.

- Don't forward abusive texts or emails or images to anyone. You could be breaking the law just by forwarding them. If they are about you, keep them as evidence. If they are about someone else, delete them and don't reply to the sender.

- Don't ever give out passwords to your mobile or email account.

- Remember that sending abusive or threatening messages is against the law.

# Victims and teachers working together

Pupils who are bullied are unable to concentrate on their schoolwork. A few are physically hurt, many are psychologically damaged. The lesson that they learn may toughen them up but it may equally well make them believe that adults just don't care about pupils. If that is not sufficient reason for doing something about school bullying, then consider this poignant plea from a 12-year-old girl:

*People just go against me in everything I say, and laugh at me. In science I said something and everyone laughed except my best friend Linda, who helps me out when they make a fool of me. They call me K9 Keenan. That hurts me very much. I get very upset. I tried to tell my mum but she told me to tell a teacher – but I just can't. Please help me.*

Despite what simplistic newspaper reports might suggest, dealing with bullying effectively does not require teachers to make a choice between paternalistic strategies that focus on adult interventions and liberal strategies that emphasise pupil involvement. Both have their place: for example, constant adult supervision and direction is vital if we are to protect vulnerable 5-year-olds in the playground but similar interventions would be given short shrift by 15-year-olds.

The following true case study shows how pupils can be given genuine responsibilities, and therefore a sense of ownership of school policies, at the same time as adults exercise their duty of care.

## Case study

John Aitkenhead founded Kilquhanity School in 1940. With his wife Morag, he ran it for more than 50 years. He died in 1998. Although inspired by A. S. Neill's Summerhill, Kilquhanity soon developed a distinctive character of its own. Unlike Summerhill, lessons were compulsory – and so was the weekly council meeting. Staff and pupils were summoned to the purpose-built circular building at 1.55 pm every Thursday. By 2.00 pm everyone was in place and the meeting began on time.

One particular meeting turned out to be especially interesting. It was chaired, extremely ably and efficiently, by a teenage girl. The secretary was also a pupil. No one was allowed to speak until invited to do so by the chair. Pupils were able to raise any matter that was concerning them.

On this occasion an 11-year-old boy complained that some older boys had been teasing him. Two admitted it and said they were sorry – but with little conviction. There seemed a danger that the matter would be glossed over but some of the other pupils (mostly older girls) described how the boys constantly teased the younger one about his hair and clothes. →

Even though the staff had to wait their turn to speak, they were able to play a very significant part, pointing out that it is not good enough just to apologise without meaning it. Morag Aitkenhead became angry at some of the older boys, who seemed to think that a fuss was being made about nothing. In her words:

*We must recognise that it took a lot of bravery for ... to say that he was being teased and no one should ridicule him for this. This is one of the most central things to this school – everyone must feel this is a good place for them and that they are happy in it.*

What was a comparatively minor case of bullying was dealt with at some length. John asked the bullying pupils to consider why they had behaved as they had. Other pupils expressed dissatisfaction with their explanations. Eventually the boys were prompted to make a more fulsome apology and a promise to stop the teasing. Although outnumbered by pupils, the teachers had been able to show their dislike of aggressive behaviour, but it was a pupil who eventually suggested that bullying could become a regular agenda item, just like laundry and breakages.

The next point that was raised showed that the meetings did not always go smoothly. Some older pupils challenged John Aitkenhead to explain a decision he had made with regard to a member of staff. John declined to do so because:

*Adult decisions are not always well understood by kids. This is a matter concerning professional ethics – I don't mind being asked but I don't think I should answer.*

In the ensuing discussion the pupils accused John of being a dictator and of pretending that the school was a democracy when it was not. Morag explained that she saw the school as being like a family and sometimes parents had to take tough decisions which they could not explain but which were, nevertheless, in their pupils' best interests. John conceded that the school was not a true democracy but was a good training for democracy.

The pupils had been able to express their dissent in a forceful way and they had been courteously listened to. But they had explored, and reached, the limits of the power of the school's council.

Consulting pupils does not mean that teachers have to lose all their authority. Giving pupils a voice does not destroy a school's hierarchy, but it does make it more accountable.

# Conclusion

If helping the victims of bullying is so difficult, if it requires schools to make a fundamental re-evaluation of policy, why bother? Such thoughts probably explain why bullying was largely ignored for so long. That, and the fact that it was difficult for teachers to provide a non-violent role model for pupils when the normal method of punishment for serious offences was the cane or the strap. But now that shadow has been lifted there is the opportunity for teachers to work with parents and pupils to minimise bullying.

We are moving into a phase where the initial media attention given to bullying is waning and schools are faced with the task of consolidating the gains that have been made, while maintaining the search for better solutions. Luckily teachers can now benefit from a wealth of literature about bullying and can draw on the expertise of organisations like Kidscape, ChildLine and the Anti-Bullying Network. Even if the problems still appear intractable, we must constantly remind ourselves what can happen to victims. A few are driven to the edge of despair and beyond. The great majority suffer less obvious, but nonetheless, serious consequences.

## Going further

**Useful websites**

www.antibullying.net

www.childline.org.uk

www.kidscape.org.uk

# Chapter 9

# Helping pupils who bully

*Michele Elliott*

## What this chapter will explore:

- Why pupils bully
- Types of bully
- Changing bullying behaviour
- The reformed bully

We know that most pupils and even adults bully others at some time. It is an unacceptable behaviour and we usually nip it in the bud by admonishment or sanctions such as losing privileges, but sometimes it gets out of hand. That is when you need to take strong and immediate action to protect your pupils and to protect yourself. And if you can help the bully change, it makes life better for the bully and easier for you.

# Why pupils bully

There are many reasons why a pupil might bully others. Pupils who bully can be high spirited, active and energetic. They may be easily bored, or envious or insecure. They may also be secure pupils who just like getting their own way and who may have become 'heroes' with the other pupils for the way they behave. They may be spoilt brats, overindulged and undisciplined.

Bullies might also be jealous of another's academic or sporting success or they may be jealous of a sibling or new baby at home. They may have a learning disability, which makes them angry and frustrated (though this may have the opposite effect and make them a target for bullies instead).

## Case study

Callum (8) became the scourge of the school playground and of his own neighbourhood. He was bullying pupils left, right and centre. His parents had been phoned by his class teacher and by the neighbours so many times that they lost count. They were in despair. They tried hitting Callum, yelling at him, taking away his pocket money, all to no avail. When his parents and teacher contacted Kidscape, Callum was well on the way to being the child from hell.

So what did his teacher and parents do? The first thing they did was to lay down the ground rules to Callum. It was made clear what would happen if he broke the rules. Everyone knew what was what.

The first time Callum tried to bully someone else he found out the school was serious. There were immediate consequences and Callum did not like them. He sat with his teacher at lunch time and was allowed to read but not interact with the other pupils. It took about two weeks of consistent consequences for him to decide it was not worth the effort to bully.

The teacher role-played with Callum ways to act with other pupils, and his parents tried to do the same at home. The teacher advised them to be consistent and to praise his good behaviour, as well as to go to the neighbours and explain that they were working on changing Callum's behaviour. They asked for patience but to let them know immediately if there was a problem.

Then Callum's parents had a talk with him when they were calm and before anything happened again. They told him that they did not expect him to bully people and that, if he did, he would be staying at home and not allowed to go out in the neighbourhood for that day. He would be allowed to go out the next day to try to be nice. But every time he bullied he would be back in the house. The hitting as punishment was stopped, at the recommendation of his teacher. It had not helped and probably made things worse since Callum was furious about being hit and took out his anger on the other pupils.

Callum's teacher asked him to explain what it was that had led up to the bullying. Evidently the other pupils teased Callum about his ears and, when they did, he blew his top. His teacher made it her business to catch out pupils making these comments and to stop it happening.

The teacher suggested to Callum's parents that Callum could try asking one boy, who seemed to like Callum, over to play some games, and then bring in the other pupils little by little.

Eventually Callum stopped bullying because he felt more confident, and the other pupils stopped making fun of him. His parents were better able to cope because they handled the situation when there was no heat or anger. Callum understood exactly where he stood and what would happen if he transgressed. And Callum's parents were able to help him because they understood his hurt feelings about the taunting.

## TOP TIP!

*Bullies may act out of anger and frustration. If you can identify the trigger point, you can help bullies to learn to recognise what sets them off. Then find ways to help them deal with it.*

# Types of bully

You already know that not all bullies are the same – sometimes a perfectly great pupil will suddenly start bullying. At other times a pupil may come into your class as a bully and just keep on bullying. There are many ways to classify bullies, including the following:

- Impulsive bullies, who have trouble keeping control of their tempers.
- Unintentional bullies, who don't realise that what they did was bullying.
- Sadistic bullies, who have no empathy and are covering up their own feelings of inadequacy.

- Imitative bullies, who are influenced by those around them.
- Group bullies, who use their collective power to intimidate.

If you look online and put in 'types of bullies' you will get more than 50 ways to classify them. To simplify it for teaching purposes, let's look at two broad types.

## Occasional bullies

The pupil who bullies out of the blue quite often has been a victim of bullying themselves – they lash out because they cannot stand it any longer. Unfortunately, when this happens you might not know the history and find yourself confronted by a miserable, hurt pupil who is not really a bully at all. Finding out all the facts will probably uncover the reason why your pupil has mysteriously turned into a bully. It may also be that the pupil is having a 'bad day' and an apology will end the problem.

Pupils may suddenly become bullies when they:

- are jealous of a brother or sister or other pupils;
- are under stress because of schoolwork or exam pressure;
- are worried about a problem that has cropped up at home, such as a pet dying;
- have problems at home, such as parents fighting or separating, a favourite sibling leaving home, a bereavement or money problems;
- have had a quarrel with a friend;
- are bored;
- are frustrated at having been bullied without it being found out;
- have had a day when everything has gone wrong.

Any of these difficulties might trigger bullying behaviour in a pupil who normally behaves well with other pupils.

### Why not try this?

A pupil who bullies only once or very occasionally is not difficult to help. Of course, they need firm guidelines and telling off, and they need to make amends for their behaviour. Try to:

- Remain calm and in control.
- Find out all the facts, including the actions of the other pupils involved.
- Discuss the problem with your pupil – it may help just to talk it over.
- Find out if the pupil is upset, worried, jealous, or has been bullied.

- Find out if the pupil knows what harm they are causing.

- Sort things out with the victim.

- Emphasise that bullying is not acceptable in any circumstances and that it will not be tolerated.

- Give your pupil some goals to behave better and reward good behaviour.

- Work out some alternative ways in which the pupil could react if the situation occurs again, such as:

  – going to a 'time-out room' in which to cool off

  – walking away

  – deep breathing

  – counting to 10.

- Give the pupil plenty of praise and encouragement if they don't repeat the bullying and are able to use some of the alternative responses.

- Determine whether the pupil needs help coping with a crisis and whether you need to involve the parents or a school counsellor (if you have one).

## Chronic bullies

Some pupils go from incident to incident, from school to school, bullying and hurting others. You could call them serial bullies, or they may be sadistic, or have any number of problems. These pupils may eventually end up being excluded from mainstream education if they continue with this behaviour. Many of them have some characteristics or backgrounds in common. They may:

- act aggressively much of the time;
- be unable to control themselves;
- have a positive attitude towards violence;
- feel insecure;
- be disruptive;
- blame the victims for the bullying (i.e. 'He looked at me funny – he deserved to be thumped');
- have no empathy with anyone;
- be bullied by family members;
- be scapegoats in the family (i.e. blamed for everything, even if it isn't their fault);

- feel under tremendous pressure to succeed when, in fact, they are failing;
- have poor social skills;
- feel different, stupid or inadequate;
- come from a 'culture of violence' in the home.

Chronic bullies may also be overindulged to the point of being worshipped by their parents, and expect that everyone should bow to their wishes. Even though these pupils are more difficult to deal with, there will still be some things you can do to help.

Keep in mind that reforming the behaviour of a chronic bully is not easy; power may be the only language they understand. Significantly, when schools organise meetings to discuss the problem of bullying, it is usually the parents of the victim who turn up, not the parents of the bully, who find it more difficult to accept change.

# Changing bullying behaviour

Once you have dealt with the immediate fall-out from the latest bullying incident, you are ready to begin on the long-term task of helping the bully to change so that they develop other non-bullying ways of behaving and reacting. This is a lengthy, time-consuming process with no guarantees of success, but you can make a difference if you give it time.

There are no definitive solutions or strategies for changing a bully's behaviour that *always* work. Each bully is an individual with their own problems and there is no general 'cure' for bullying. If possible, working with the bully's parents makes progress much faster, but you may not have their cooperation. Even without it, these successful ideas from teachers might be worth a try.

## Peer pressure

Peer pressure is one of the most effective ways of stamping out bullying. Pupils will stop bullying among themselves after discussions, role-plays, drawing up and signing contracts, and understanding what is and what is not acceptable behaviour. If a peer mentoring system is put in place you will probably see that bullies will pull back because they have lost their appreciative audience (see Chapter 13).

## Unexpected drop-in

Drop by the lunchroom or playground without telling your pupils. Have a look for bullying behaviour, especially on the part of the bullies you are helping. We know that pupils are good at acting like angels in our sight, but seeing them in an unstructured environment will give you a better idea of their behaviour. Get other staff to let you know about any bullying behaviour they may observe – for example, during PE.

## Expectations

Discuss with bullies the behaviour that you expect. Give clear guidelines about their behaviour. This will help to eliminate any future misunderstandings. (For example, 'If you do this again, then you will not be going on the school journey. Alternatively if you behave, you will be allowed to go.')

## Admit, atone, apologise

Before you can begin to change a bully's behaviour, they need to *admit* that what they have done is wrong. They must *admit* that their behaviour has been hurtful and unkind. They have to realise that they owe the victim an *apology* and they should try to *atone* for what they have done.

The bully may apologise, however grudgingly, and hand back stolen items or money, without feeling any remorse, only anger that they have been 'found out'. This does not mean the apology is totally meaningless. It is merely a starting point and is one way of bringing home to the pupil that what they have done is wrong and unacceptable.

## Short-term goals

Discuss the next steps and set realistic short-term goals. Make sure that these goals are attainable, even if you set something simple like no bullying for the day, or morning, or even for 30 minutes if the pupil has little control. Try to work something out with the pupil's parents or caretakers as well. It is better to give a pupil an easy target, even if you think it ludicrously simple, because this virtually guarantees success. The object is to make the pupil feel good about achieving self-control.

## Break the pattern

If the pupil is often involved in bully incidents, find out if there is a pattern to the bullying. It is helpful to keep a record of every bullying incident, either with an online monitoring system mentioned in Chapter 2, or by hand. You will want to know:

● How long has the bullying been going on?
● Do particular situations provoke the pupil?
● Is there one victim or does the bully target several pupils?

The answers to these questions will help you to identify what is triggering the bullying. Perhaps the bullying happens at lunch or in the playground. Maybe the bully gets frustrated and acts out because they cannot do a particular subject or they are having trouble learning to read. Ask the pupil to come up with three ways to deal with their anger.

## Why not try this?

If you have the time, ask the pupil who is bullying others to take a piece of paper and draw a line down the middle. Put a title at the top: 'Why I Bully'. On the left-hand side ask the pupil to write the reasons they bully; on the right-hand side ask for solutions from the pupil and/or from yourself.

The following ideas are from pupils and are just a tiny sample. You will find that pupils who bully may not know why they bully, but this may start to give them and you insight that can lead to behaviour change.

| Why I bully | Suggestions from pupil (or teacher) |
|---|---|
| Boredom | ● Take on more responsibility |
| | ● Get involved with more activities |
| | ● Find work more suited to my ability |
| Revenge | ● Examine why and find better ways to express myself |
| | ● Work out whether it's because I was bullied |
| Jealousy | ● Find something I am good at |
| | ● Stop comparing myself to others |
| | ● Find something I can do well |
| Status | ● Work out what the status is based on – fear, violence? |
| | ● Think of other ways, e.g. as a good athlete, writer, wood-worker, mechanic, dancer, singer |
| Anger | ● Work on what makes me angry – doing poorly in maths or reading or PE – and get help to do better |

Gain

- Try getting away from my fighting parents by staying at school later, visiting relatives or friends, going into my room and playing music
- Take up martial arts
- Accept that being a thief is not the best way because I get in trouble [not a lot of insight about the effect on the victims]
- Role-play having my money stolen and discussing how it feels
- Get a job like mowing lawns, cleaning, paper round

It's fun

- Think of better ways to have fun – fishing, gardening, music, art, helping little kids learn to read

## Clear guidelines

Draw up some clear behaviour guidelines on how you expect the pupil to behave in future. If the pupil does not know acceptable ways of behaving, they may need some very basic information about generally accepted standards of behaviour. For example, 'When you talk to other people, smile, look them in the eyes and act in a pleasant manner. Now let's try it. You pretend that I am someone you have met or want to eat lunch with.' Then act out the parts and praise the pupil for getting it right.

I have found that teachers who set up consistent rules and stick to them actually help bullies to change their behaviour. Interestingly, some of these pupils continue to act out at home or in their neighbourhoods but not in school. They are quite capable of discovering what is acceptable in different settings. You probably already see that with your own pupils – some respond to strict rules, others to a more laid-back approach. From my experience with bullies, they seem to react better when they know exactly where they stand and what you expect (that approach worked best with my own sons as well as in my classroom).

## Self-esteem

Many bullies have low self-esteem. Try giving the pupil extra responsibilities. Give them plenty of praise and encouragement when they behave well or complete tasks successfully. This helps build up their self-esteem. It may be that you ask the pupil to help with younger pupils by listening to them reading or reading a story to them. Or ask the pupil to devise a quiz about bullying, or perhaps think of ways that cyberbullying can be tackled.

**Why not try this?**

If the bully is active, boisterous and quick-tempered, you can try to divert that excess energy into useful activities. Get the pupil to help with physical tasks — fetching and carrying jobs, putting up posters, stacking chairs, moving books, tidying the classroom, going on errands, getting equipment ready — basically anything that gets them moving in a positive way. Give lots of praise and rewards. Bullies need to feel they are good at something besides bullying.

## Freeze the action

Discuss with the bully what sort of situations make them flare up and then help them find other ways of reacting. Make up some simple role-plays based on what the bully has told you or about situations you have observed. Ask the pupil to play themselves and 'freeze' the action at the point where they usually lash out or start challenging others. Ask the pupil to think about other ways of behaving such as walking away, deep breathing, or going to a 'time-out room' to cool off.

## Assertive v. aggressive

Explain the difference between aggressive and assertive behaviour. Work out verbal responses that are assertive rather than aggressive. For example, 'Stop kicking my chair *now* or I will punch you' could be replaced with 'Could you please stop that.' Simple short responses are best.

## Increase awareness

If the bully does not know or understand about the pain and suffering their actions cause, give them a copy of the letter from the bully at the end of this chapter and discuss it with them. Get them to write a similar letter.

You can also use role-plays to give bullies a chance to empathise with victims. Get the bully to role-play being a victim and ask them to discuss how they feel in this role. This might bring out the information that the pupil is a bully because they themselves have been bullied.

Other ways of helping might include professional counselling or finding out if the pupil has a learning disability or medical condition that is exacerbating their behaviour. Parents will obviously have to be involved for this to happen.

## Supervision

This may not be possible, given the shortage of staff in schools, but it does help if you are able to assign a teacher or another staff member to monitor the bully. This person acts as a safety-valve for the pupil – someone they can talk to if they feel a bullying incident 'coming on'. Clearly, work and time pressures may make this strategy impossible, but it can be extremely helpful and actually cut down on the amount of time spent trying to curb the bully's behaviour.

I heard of one mother who decided to supervise her child herself. With the cooperation of the school, she sat in on his classes and watched him in the playground and in the lunchroom. The boy vowed after one day of this that he would never bully anyone again.

**TOP TIP!**

*Make sure anti-bullying training is in place for those in charge of school buses. One 11-year-old boy, Ben, hanged himself after the pupils and the bus driver picked on him.*

**Why not try this?**

Ask the pupil to think about changes they would like to make. This might be specific, like changing behaviour in the lunchroom or on the bus. Or it could be a general change of behaviour, such as stopping acting like a bully. Decide together on a time scale for the change and draw up a clear plan of action. For example:

● Tomorrow I will go into the lunchroom [on the bus, into PE, etc.] and I will ...

● From now on, when I start to feel like punching someone [or sending a nasty text or cyberbullying] I will ...

# The reformed bully

Sometimes, if pupils know that a bully is trying to 'reform', they will try to provoke the bully into displaying their old, aggressive behaviour and will tease and taunt them until they lose control and react angrily. Be on the look out for this sort of baiting and be aware of comments designed to goad the behaving pupil into bullying.

Do not expect instant results. It can take a term or the entire year to change a persistent bully's behaviour and there are likely to be many setbacks along the way. But it is worth the effort if you can find the time to work with the bully to help them to change.

## TOP TIP!

Don't make a mountain out of a molehill. Some bullying incidents are one-off misunderstandings, which the pupils themselves will settle without your intervention.

## Case study

A couple of years ago, I received this handwritten letter in the post with no name or address. You can show it to all pupils to discuss or to the pupil who is bullying others. Just let them know that it is a real letter from a real person who grew up to regret her behaviour. You could also give them the letter and leave out the last paragraph and ask them to write a conclusion.

*I don't really know how to explain things. I never even realised how awful I was at school until I was at least 22. One day one of the managers at work told me that his daughter had been at the same school as me. She used to dread meeting me at school and she said that I was well known as the school bully. I'd never really admitted to myself that what I did was bullying – it was just a bit of fun as far as I was concerned. I was embarrassed that the manager talked to me. I wanted to drop through the floor. But it made me think about what I had done all those years ago.*

*It's not that my childhood was so awful. Yes, my parents were always fighting, and my bother picked on me all the time. But I guess lots of kids have stories like that to tell about their lives. I really didn't have much excuse to do what I did, but I liked the feeling of power that bullying gave me. No one messed with me!*

*I think the bullying started when somebody upset me in the Infants and some of the boys showed me how to make a fist and 'sort her out'. I suppose I just carried on from there. I never used a gang for support and I picked on boys and girls – it didn't matter who they were. I'd lie in wait for them on the way home. I used to cat-call and fight them – not just pulling hair and scratching, but real fighting. I even knocked a girl out once. I was never beaten. Perhaps I would have stopped if somebody had been able to beat me.*

*I always had an excuse for why I bullied. Things like 'they were snobs' or 'they'd hurt me', but I know they were pathetic excuses. The lads used to egg me on as well, but even when we moved to another area I still carried on. The bullying went on until I left school.*

*I used to feel a rush whenever I got at someone. I seemed to get satisfaction from knowing that I'd hurt and beaten others. At heart, I was scared. I thought nobody liked me. I thought I was ugly. I had a big nose and the boys all used to tease me. I felt very insecure about how I looked, but then again lots of people feel that way and never bully others.*

*I discovered how to bully people using texts and emails. I got 'friends' to take photos and videos with their mobiles while I hit and kicked pupils. I sat in the back of the school bus and always had a victim – kids used to do anything to avoid sitting next to me, that is most kids. But the kids who laughed and egged me on loved me, or so I thought. They didn't care, they just wanted a bit of excitement and I was too stupid to see that. I thought the other kids liked me because they hung around and cheered when I was bullying.*

*I am writing to you in the hope that some young bully might read this and change his or her ways before it is too late. Now I feel really bad about what I did, but I wonder if any of my victims will ever know?*

## Conclusion

When you work with bullies, you need to intervene as soon as you can. Explain clearly what you expect and make sure that bullies admit, apologise and atone for their behaviour. Working with the bully, discuss and set goals, both short and long term, but also set sanctions for bullying behaviour, such as time out, missing a school outing, eating or having break time alone, or even writing lines – anything that works. At the same time, remember always to reward and praise good behaviour. To help the bully to change their behaviour, encourage them to practise ways to stop reacting to a situation by bullying. Suggest ways to try to control their aggression by exercises such as walking away, counting to 10 and deep breathing, or positive activities such as sports, drama, music and art.

# Working with parents
## *Michele Elliott*

**What this chapter will explore:**

- Working with parents of bullied pupils
- Working with parents of bullies
- Options for parents

Most parents are involved and interested in the education of their children and will be happy to meet you throughout the school year in various situations. The dynamics can change when bullying occurs. Then the parents of the bullied pupil and also the parents of the bully will be unsure about what is happening to their child and uncertain about how you will react.

# Working with parents of bullied pupils

Some parents have no problem contacting you to talk about their concerns that their child is being bullied. Others may be scared to get in touch with you or anyone at the school because they:

- found out that their child is being bullied and the child has pleaded with them not to tell you;
- are scared to talk to teachers (you would be surprised how many parents find you and the whole school situation intimidating);
- were bullied themselves when they were in school and are devastated that it is happening to their child;
- are afraid of the bullies and the families of the bullies;
- think nothing will be done and the bullying will only get worse;
- are ashamed that their child is not succeeding socially;
- feel they are bad parents.

## Case study

Erin (13) waited until the last week of term to tell her mother, a primary teacher, about the bullying that had gone on for most of the year. For some reason, which Erin could not figure out, she had been the target of a group of 16-year-old girls. These girls had followed her home after school, emailed her, set up a website and downloaded doctored photos, made her friends stop talking to her and generally made her life absolutely miserable. Erin spent her lunch time in the library and avoided going out during breaks.

Erin was a very pretty girl, intelligent and hard working. She had never encountered bullying before and was shocked and surprised that she was the target of so much hatred. It is not surprising that the bullies were marginal pupils, but they were popular, pretty girls. These pupils had no need to be jealous of Erin or to embark on this bullying campaign. It turned out that one of the girls, Alice, thought Erin was after her boyfriend (untrue) and that was the start of the whole mess. Instead of finding out the facts, Alice decided to attack Erin and to get her friends to join in. Such was Alice's clout with pupils that no one questioned her when she announced that Erin had been spreading rumours and 'needed sorting out'.

The only reason Erin finally told about the bullying was because she felt safe – these girls were leaving school at the end of term and Erin had held on as long as she could. What upset Erin's mother most was that it seemed no one at school realised that these girls were bullying her daughter. How could that be?

To be fair to the school, in this case the bullies had been very clever and managed to pull off their stunts when there were no staff around. And Erin had not told anyone except her best friend, whom she had sworn to secrecy. Without this friend, Erin probably would have cracked under the strain. As it was, she continued to do well in most of her subjects and hide the pain she was in.

When Erin's mother said she would go to see the teacher, Erin cried and pleaded with her not to go.

- Had you been Erin's teacher, what signs might have alerted you to the bullying?
- If Erin's mother came to see you, how could you work together to help Erin?

As mentioned in Chapter 2, it is not unusual for bullied pupils to try to hide what is happening. They beg parents not to talk to teachers, and by the time the parent does approach you the bullying may be severe and much more difficult to deal with than had you known earlier. But if the bullying is happening at school then you need to do something about it. Some parents try to work with their children alone, but that rarely solves the problem.

## TOP TIP!

*In your letter and email home to parents about your school policy on bullying (see Chapter 13), put in a sentence about contacting you if they find out their child is being bullied. Suggest they ask their child to think about who would be the best person to talk to if they are worried about bullying at school.*

## Why not try this?

In discussions about bullying with your pupils, make it plain that you want them to tell you if they are being bullied. Give them the case of Erin above and ask them what they think Erin's mother should do now. This will give you some insight into how your pupils think about the cooperation between school and home. One young person I dealt with said he would never want his parent to come into school because it would seem he was not capable of handling things himself.

## Case study

So what happened in the case of Erin? Erin's mother decided that she should let the teacher know that the bullying had gone on, even if the bullies were leaving the school. After all, perhaps there were other victims, and why should the bullies be allowed to get away with their behaviour? Erin argued that she would not have told her mother if she thought her mother would go to the school. After several days of debate and heated discussions, they compromised. Erin's mother would talk to a teacher Erin liked, but only after the bullies left the school at the end of term.

Erin's teacher felt badly that he had not spotted the bullying, especially since he had seen her in the library every day instead of in the lunchroom. Erin went on to have a good experience for the rest of her time at the school and slowly rebuilt her confidence.

It is too bad that the teacher was not told earlier as it would have given Erin a chance to see that the staff would have helped her. Also, the girls who were bullying her needed to be pulled up short for the way they had behaved. They left that school knowing they had hoodwinked everyone and got away with it. It cannot be good for their characters that they succeeded in bullying. It is a shame that Erin's mother, as a teacher herself, could not persuade Erin to let her talk to her teacher.

## Practical strategies

Here are some strategies that can help when you are contacted by an anxious or angry parent because of suspected bullying:

- Set up a meeting at the earliest opportunity. Include the pupil if appropriate.
- Make sure you set the tone by being calm, by listening and by being supportive.
- Do not try to get the families of the alleged victim and alleged bully together before knowing as much as possible about them. (In the school where I was a governor for 15 years, we had the mother of the bully sink her teeth into the father of the victim. You live and learn ...)
- Try to hold the meeting when other pupils are not around, so the victim can feel safe talking to you.
- Make the meeting informal in the first instance.
- You may want another staff member present, but try not to make the meeting seem like the Spanish Inquisition for the parent coming in.
- If the parent is a single parent, invite them to bring along a friend.

- Remember that parents may be distressed, worried, fearful and angry, but the one thing they will want to know is whether you take this issue seriously and will try to do something about it.

Before the meeting, make sure you have your anti-bullying policy to hand so that you can give it to the parents if they need it. You would be amazed at the tales parents tell about trying to see their school's anti-bullying policy: 'They said it was in a file somewhere and they would send it to me – that was three months ago and they just keep coming up with excuses'; 'I was told it would cost me £3 to get a copy'; 'Put your request in writing'; and my favourite – 'The policy is confidential for health and safety reasons.' You can imagine how frustrated these parents must be when met with silly excuses and delaying tactics while they are worried sick about their child.

Anti-bullying policies should be available everywhere. This avoids bad feelings and parents thinking you have something to hide.

Having set up a meeting with the victim's parents, what next?

- Collect as much information from the parents as possible.
- If the pupil is very distressed, suggest that the parents consult their GP.
- Try to find out if the pupil has threatened suicide. If so, not only should the parents take the child to their GP but you should also talk to your headteacher.
- Agree a timeline when you will get back to the parents.
- Consult with the appropriate staff member. Some schools have a designated 'bully liaison teacher' or counsellor.
- Observe what is happening in the playground, in the lunchroom, gym, classroom, halls, on the school bus, etc.
- Talk to your colleagues and ask them to keep an eye out for this particular child.
- If you have pupils who are mature, discrete and reliable, ask if they know anything about a bullying situation going on – don't mention names. This works best if you have a peer mentoring or buddy system in place (see Chapter 11).
- Keep a record of what is agreed and when you need to contact the parents again.
- Keep parents informed of progress. If you are still looking into things, ring the parents and tell them. That way they will know you are still on the case.

**TOP TIP!**

*What parents need to hear is that the bullying will be dealt with and that their child will feel safe to come to school.*

**TOP TIP!**

*Refrain from saying anything about the alleged bully or bully's family to the parents of the alleged victim. You may find the parents want the bully expelled immediately and are looking to you to accomplish this. They may also want information about the bully which, of course, you cannot give. Keep the meeting focused on the concerns and suggestions being made by the parents and how you can work together.*

## The whole picture

While it is probably true that bullying is a problem for the pupil, the reality is that what is presented to you may not be completely straightforward. The picture presented to the parents by their child may be overstated or understated, or not true, or be a symptom of some other problem. There could be family difficulties, a pending divorce or the death of a beloved grandparent, or dozens of other reasons that have nothing to do with bullying. Ask the parents if there is anything you need to know that will help you to help their child.

It may also be that the pupil complaining about bullying is misinterpreting everyday banter without malice as bullying. One suggestion is to ask the parents and pupil to keep a record of what is happening, with times, dates and names (if they are willing to name names). Older pupils will probably want to do this on their own without parental input. The purpose is to see if a pattern emerges about who is bullying, and when and where the bullying is happening at school. It may be that you can then look out for what is going on and make a judgement about the seriousness of the bullying. In most cases I have found that parents taking the time and trouble to come in to talk to you means that the bullying is perceived as harming their child. In a few situations it becomes clear that the real problem has nothing to do with the other pupils but with the home issues that have made the child such a wreck that they think everyone is a bully.

## Take a break

There are times when it is best for a pupil to take a break from school for their own mental health. Some teachers feel it is best that pupils do not do this; personally, having sat with parents whose children have committed suicide because of bullying at school, I would suggest it is wise always to err on the side of caution.

---

**Why not try this?**

One excellent teacher I knew used the following calming statements when parents requested a meeting with her about bullying:

- Let's make an appointment right now – when can you come in? Let's work together to sort this out as soon as possible.

- I know you are worried but try not to react in a way that makes your child think it is better to retract than for you to talk to me. This is because so many pupils do not want parents to 'interfere' as they think it will make matters worse (and it sometimes does).

- If there is time before our meeting, sit and write down everything you can about the bullying that has happened so far and bring it with you. Make sure that you put in as many times, dates and names as you can find out.

- Make out a list of points you want to cover in the meeting.

- I am looking forward to working with you.

She used her wonderful people skills to ensure harmony and she managed to stop and prevent most bullying in her class. Remember her five simple statements when you have to deal with a distressed parent.

---

## Supporting the parents

The way to ensure that parents become even more annoyed or anxious about bullying is to ignore their concerns or fob them off. In a survey for Kidscape, these were the responses that parents said drove them to despair:

- 'I will ring you back' – but it never happens.

- 'I can see you in two weeks' – way too long.

- 'Your child is too sensitive' – maybe, but how does that help solve the problem?

- 'The bully has problems that you should try to understand' – why should their child suffer because another child has problems?

- 'If your child doesn't like it here, you can remove them; we have a waiting list' – a reply from fee-paying and religious schools.

Thinking about bullying from a parental viewpoint, what would you like to be said to you and how would you like the teacher to react to your concerns?

## Working with parents of bullies

This is a tough one. Once you have found out as much information as possible from colleagues, pupils and observation, you may have to contact the parents of the alleged bully. If you have previously talked to the parents and know that they are cooperative and want their child to stop bullying, then it is a matter of reassuring them that you want to continue to help them help their child using some of the techniques in Chapter 9. Remember, too, that their child may be an unintentional bully.

If you have to contact the parents of a bully, you may be unsure about how they will react. Here are some strategies that can help:

- Discuss the situation with your colleagues or headteacher before contacting the parents.
- Ask another colleague to sit with you when you make the first telephone call.
- Write or email and ask for a meeting or telephone conversation.
- Have all the points you want to make written down so that you can refer to them if necessary.
- Remain as calm and as friendly as possible, without being subservient.
- Listen carefully without interrupting.
- Do not accuse, just state the facts as you know them.
- Make sure you are seated and that the parent is not standing over you – this gives you equal status.
- Try to have something positive to say about their child and how you value their input.
- Use silence and patience instead of argument. It is effective and often stops aggressive verbal diatribe.
- Use reflective listening statements like, 'It seems that you are very upset by this' or 'This must be difficult.'
- Try to be dispassionate and do not get caught up in the anger or emotions of the parents. They may not believe their child is capable of bullying and are addressing their feelings at you, though you are not the cause of their anger.
- If possible build a relationship with the parents, saying that you and they only want what is best for their child and that you will try to help.

- Set boundaries such as, 'I would like to talk with you now but I have a class to teach. May I ring you after school and we can talk for longer and try to sort this out?'

- Do not allow a parent to bully or threaten you. Do not react, but calmly stand up and say, 'We need to work together. Let's meet again. Thank you for letting me know how you feel about this.'

> **TOP TIP!**
>
> It is a waste of time to argue with parents about bullying. You could say something like: 'I appreciate your concern and will discuss it with the headteacher' or 'Let's talk tomorrow so we can both think of ways to go forward.'

Remember that you are not a punch bag or doormat for a difficult parent. It certainly helps you to understand why your pupil is bullying others, but there is no excuse for you to take the parent's abuse. In any event, the parent's attitude is displaced anger that should not be directed at you.

## Setting up meetings

Often these bullying situations arise out of nowhere and you need to see parents or caretakers quickly. So try to think in advance about how to set up a meeting so that everyone is comfortable:

- Arrange the room where you talk to parents so that you are close to the door and can leave if necessary.
- Try not to sit behind a desk so it does not seem like you are creating barriers.
- Leave the door open and make sure there are other people within calling distance.
- Prepare what you want to accomplish and have bullet-point notes.
- Start the meeting with a statement of the time you expect to take: 'I know how busy you are and we have 30 minutes, so let's see what we can do together.'
- Agree on the way forward and follow it up with a note or email.
- Set the time and date for your next meeting.
- Stand up, shake hands, look them in the eyes and thank them for coming or for their cooperation (if it ends well).

Not all parents of pupils who are bullies will come to a meeting in an aggressive mood, but it is better to be prepared and happily surprised than be caught off guard. Unfortunately, difficult parents are out there and it would be a miracle if you escaped seeing any in your career.

> **Why not try this?**
>
> If you have no experience in meeting with parents to talk about bullying, ask a friend or colleague to do a brief role-play, with you as the teacher and them as the parent. Use the following two scenarios, tailored to the age of pupils you teach:
>
> - The parent of a severely bullied pupil comes in to see you. His son is so distressed by a group of boys who are bullying him that he does not want to come to school. You have not seen anything suspicious.
>
> - The parent of a pupil who has a history of bad behaviour comes in at your request to talk about the latest victim of her child's aggression. She does not believe her child is a bully and she thinks that the school is always picking on her child, 'who is no angel, but…'.

# Options for parents

Parents have the right to take their concerns further if they feel the bullying of their child has not been dealt with to their satisfaction. This is not necessarily dissatisfaction with you but with the system. The information for parents about what else they can do should be in your school's anti-bullying policy. You can also tell parents that if they are not satisfied:

- they can start by making an appointment with the headteacher;
- if they are still unhappy, they can contact the board of governors;
- if that does not work, they can contact the local authority and complain in writing;
- finally they can also write to the Secretary of State for Education.

Although very few complaints go this far, it is good that you know how they are handled in your school and by your local authority.

## Involving the GP

If a pupil is very upset or depressed about the bullying, some parents will take their child to their GP to try to get help. If it were your child, you might think that this is a good idea, particularly if you were worried about how the bullying was affecting their health. But not everyone agrees.

> ### Reflecting on practice
>
> ● How would you react if a pupil was given a stress break from your class?
>
> ● Would you ever suggest to a parent that they get in touch with the GP about bullying? Why or why not? What would you say?

Some GPs have given pupils a written excuse to stay away from school because of bullying. Other people think that pupils should be sent back to school, comparing it to falling off a horse – you need to get back on and keep riding. The message is that the more time you take off, the more difficult it will be to go back to school. However, we need to ask how difficult it is for a pupil to go into a bullying situation every day.

## Involving the police

In some cases, police are called because bullying may be classed as an assault. Parents have also sued schools and local authorities. A bullying incident could involve you in a court case, although at the moment this is rare.

## Media exposure

Increasingly, parents are going to the media to expose bullying cases that have not been handled well. The most heartbreaking of these cases are the parents who talk about their child having committed suicide. I have sat with more parents who have suffered the death of their child then I ever thought possible. For example, the parents of Matthew described on television how online bullying drove their 17-year-old son to kill himself just before Christmas. And 11-year-old Ben hanged himself, again just before Christmas, because of school and school bus bullying. It is tragic that something was not done, even though both sets of parents had been in contact with the schools. They were bitter because they felt their concerns were not taken seriously. Ignoring parents can have devastating consequences.

## Removing pupils from school

Parents can remove their child from your school and find another. In some cases, the pupil who was the victim of bullying in one school thrives and has no problems in the new school. You could only conclude that the problem was not with the pupil but with the school, which allowed the bullying to go on.

Many parents of bullied children decide to educate their child at home with the help of organisations like Education Otherwise (www.education-otherwise.org). The law says parents must educate their children, but it does not say it has to be done in a school setting.

Luckily, most bullying situations will never reach these later steps, partly because of your efforts to ensure that parents and teachers work together.

# Conclusion

Working with parents around issues of bullying is complex and often time consuming. Parents do not know what to expect when they talk to you. They are worried about what is happening to their child, about how you will react or cope with what they say, how they feel about having a child who is a bully or a victim of bullying, and what can be done to stop the bullying. You have the added stress of juggling the pupils and both sides of the bullying story, trying to keep everyone happy. You will not always succeed, but in the vast majority of cases, listening to and working with parents produces the best chance of preventing and stopping bullying.

## Going further

**Useful websites**

www.education-otherwise.org

www.kidscape.org.uk

www.parentlineplus.org.uk

**Books for parents**

Fried. S. and Fried, P., *Bullies and Victims – Helping Your Children Through the Schoolyard Battlefield* (M. Evans and Co., 1998).

Brown, K., *Bullying: What Can Parents Do?* (Monarch Books, 1997).

Elliott, M., *101 Ways to Deal with Bullying: A Guide for Parents* (Hodder, 1997).

# Peer support
## *Claude Knights*

**What this chapter will explore:**

- What is peer support?
- Approaches to peer support
- Setting up a peer support system
- Peer listening scheme

An effective school is concerned with the overall well-being of all pupils. A peer support system can make a vital contribution, since it helps senior pupils and staff to tackle issues like bullying in a positive and productive manner. So that senior pupils can deliver this support, a training and supervision programme must be set up in the school. It would take a whole book to describe all the various forms of peer support and the training required, so this chapter concentrates especially on one form – peer listening.

You might then feel confident to set up your own programme of peer support or want to look into the other forms and set up an alternative one. If you feel you need more training to ensure that you and your pupils have the skills necessary to carry a programme through, you can always look for peer support training. Useful sources of support and training are listed at the end of this chapter.

# What is peer support?

'Peer support' is an umbrella term, which includes different but related models that have been set up in schools across the UK. In general terms, peer support schemes provide an opportunity for pupils to share concerns and explore their own solutions to a range of issues. They build on pupils' natural willingness to seek out their peers when they are experiencing problems, and on pupils' ability to act in a genuine, empathic way towards one another.

In summary:

- Peer support is based on the fact that pupils most often seek out other pupils when they are experiencing some concern or worry.
- Peer support relies strongly on communication to encourage self-exploration and decision making.
- Peer supporters are *not* professional counsellors or therapists; they are pupils who offer supervised support to other pupils, helping them to think through and reflect on any concerns that they may be experiencing.
- Peer supporters should be given training to provide a non-judgemental, active approach to listening, which encourages others to express and explore their concerns and frustrations.
- The basis of peer support programmes is the understanding that those involved have similar characteristics to those being helped, for example in age or life experience.

Peer support schemes can therefore have a very positive influence on the emotional climate of a school. They also have an important educational value, since they allow pupils to learn much about themselves, their peers and relationships in general. Creating a framework in which pupils can support each other recognises the vital role pupils can play in making positive changes in their own lives as well as in those of friends and peers.

# Approaches to peer support

All peer support schemes aim to provide a setting in which pupils feel it is safe to talk and where they know they will be listened to. These schemes recognise that meeting the needs of the whole person will help pupils to achieve their social and academic potential.

Effective peer support systems have been set up in primary as well as in secondary school settings. From about the age of 9, most pupils have the ability to understand and empathise with the needs of others and should be able to cope with the demands of a training course. The age of the pupils and the needs of the school will determine the type and length of the training, as well as the nature of the support system chosen.

A basic training course usually covers essential elements, including:

- boundaries
- active listening and questioning skills
- confidentiality guidelines
- solution-focused approaches.

Further training for peer supporters will be determined by the objectives of the service being established. For example, if the aim is to address issues around bullying, awareness raising in this area would be essential.

There are a number of ways in which peer support can operate:

- **Peer listeners** provide a confidential service as active listeners and facilitators, providing a safe opportunity for other pupils to share their concerns and to explore possible solutions.
- **Peer mediators** are trained in conflict resolution strategies and may act as mediators in response to bullying situations.
- **Peer mentors** are often given a specific focus, such as acting as a befriender or buddy to pupils as they enter a new school. They can also provide support for pupils who are vulnerable for a variety of reasons.

Whichever model of peer support is adopted, it should be clearly defined, and the roles and responsibilities of those who are to provide the service should be understood and supported by the whole-school community. It is also vital that the approach is compatible with the school's framework of policies and procedures on issues such as anti-bullying and child protection, confidentiality and record keeping, as well as equal opportunities. When implementing the scheme:

- Clear criteria should be established for selecting the pupils who are to be peer supporters.
- The pupils should receive appropriate and ongoing training (links with other schools using the same model may be useful here).

- Peer support schemes should be monitored and evaluated regularly to ensure that objectives are being met.
- Time should be allocated for key staff to liaise with local and national support agencies.

**TOP TIP!**

*Peer support must be part of a whole-school approach that promotes a caring and positive ethos. As the peer supporters will require ongoing help and supervision, such projects involve the active commitment of more than one member of staff.*

## How can peer supporters help?

The role of peer supporters will be determined by the needs of the school, as well as the training available. Peer supporters may be involved in any of the following:

- Helping pupils with learning.
- Helping younger or new pupils make the transition to a new school.
- Assisting with topics of concern to other pupils.
- Assisting pupils in resolving disputes.
- Helping with bullying situations.
- Helping others to sort out concerns, brainstorm ideas and offer practical help.
- Reaching out to lonely or troubled pupils.

# Setting up a peer support system

**Case study**

A secondary school with 600 pupils contacted Kidscape to ask for help setting up a peer listening scheme. The school had some bullying problems and the teachers recognised that the pupils were more likely to tell each other than an adult if they were upset. However, the teachers were concerned that pupils would not know what to do with the information they received from their peers or how to give bullied pupils the help they needed. The staff were all involved in a meeting to explain the options and they chose to set up a peer listening scheme because it did not involve as much time and effort as some of the other schemes. It was a good decision for their school's needs.

Two teachers volunteered to oversee the programme and they explained to the pupils what peer listening was and that it depended upon pupils listening to and helping others make decisions. A recruitment campaign was run by pupils, and 10 peer listeners from the sixth form were chosen and trained. A room was allocated in which the trained peer listeners, working in pairs, were available during lunch and break times. Very soon, reports of bullying were reduced, attendance figures increased and the pupils and teacher declared the scheme a great success. As one of the pupils said:

> I was being bullied online and being called names. I was ashamed to tell my mother or the teachers, but it was OK to talk to the peer listener because they understood what it was like. They let me make the decisions so it wasn't like they told me what to do – that was good and I felt more confident.

A primary school with 300 pupils also contacted Kidscape and set up a buddy scheme where the pupils, after training, were on duty at playtime. The 'buddies' helped pupils get involved in games if they were on the sidelines, listened to problems and helped to create a positive atmosphere. They were trained to notice if pupils seemed sad or left out and made a great effort to include them. The 'buddies' did not patrol the playground but used their training to be alert to problems and to intervene or get help from a teacher. The teachers noted that the scheme brought the pupils together and that all the pupils seemed to watch out more for each other than they had previously. They also found that playground squabbles reduced and that the pupils managed to sort out most things themselves, freeing up teacher time.

Whatever age group you teach, once you have decided that you want to set up a peer support programme, you need to see if your colleagues are on board. You could set one up with just your class or year group if other teachers agree, but the best solution is for the entire school to be involved.

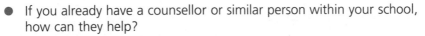

**Reflecting on practice**

So let's say everyone is interested in a peer support scheme and you are the lead teacher. Ask yourself the following questions:

- If you already have a counsellor or similar person within your school, how can they help?
- Which approach best suits your school and how much training will your pupils need? If your pupils are used to being involved in decision making or setting up school contracts (see Chapter 13) then the →

idea of letting them run a peer support programme with your help will be more readily accepted than if they are never allowed to take any decisions.

- What are your aims and how much time do you have? For example, if you have only limited time and your aim is to prevent new pupils being involved in bullying incidents, you might set up something like a peer mentoring buddy system. Older pupils are assigned to new and young pupils to help them as they move into a new class or the school. But if your aim is to get pupils to resolve general bullying conflicts, you would need considerable time to train your pupils and to be there to help. Of course you can use any type of peer support and call it whatever you wish, as long as the pupils are supported, secure and effective and you have the time to oversee them.

- Are there any resources available? Is there a room that pupils can use?

- How many hours can you be released from your other duties?

- How will other pupils know who the peer supporters are? Will they wear little pins or badges?

- When will the peer supporters be trained and where?

- How will you choose the pupils and how long will they serve?

- How long will it take to get the scheme up and running?

- If a pupil finds out something that must be told to an adult, what about confidentiality?

- How will you evaluate the effectiveness of your programme?

## TOP TIP!

Although all these things are important, it is equally important not to be put off trying to set up a peer support programme because it seems too complicated. The rewards for pupils can be numerous and many schools are successfully using various schemes.

## Peer listening scheme

So that we can concentrate on one form of peer support in more detail, let's assume that you have decided to launch a peer listening scheme. You have the support of staff and you have the resources to set up the programme, including a room where you can meet to train your pupils.

How will you select the pupils to be your peer listeners? The pupils should be:

- representative of the population of your school
- approachable
- willing to be involved.

As you select pupils for the peer listener role, you may already have in mind the kind of person you think would be effective. When a group of trained peer supporters were asked what characteristics they thought were needed, they said that the peer supporter should be:

- trustworthy
- confidential
- accepting
- understanding
- caring
- warm
- interested in people
- a good listener
- non-judgemental
- empathetic
- genuine.

That is a long list and you may not have anyone who fits all these criteria, but they are a useful guide.

## Why not try this?

It is a good idea to think about how you will recruit your peer listeners. You can make up an application form that the pupils can fill out either on paper or online. You could then have interviews in which you give the applicants bullying cases they can talk about. For example:

There is an older pupil who everyone knows is bullying young pupils. You know that the bully has made the victims too afraid to tell, but you have seen the bully push the victims around and demand their lunch money. What could you do?

Another way to set up the peer listener system is to take anyone who volunteers. The difficulty is that the bullies themselves may volunteer because they want to gain power or have a laugh. You need to decide what you would do if pupils who you know would be totally inappropriate try to become part of the programme.

Perhaps you could use those pupils you do not choose in some other way, like asking them to help with raising awareness of the peer listening programme, publicity or getting the room ready.

Once you have chosen the pupils you think would be good peer listeners, you need to begin training them. You can seek help from organisations that provide training (see the end of this chapter) or you may feel confident to devise the training yourself. The following sections outline some of the key skills you would need to develop when setting up a peer listening programme.

## Levels of listening

Peer listeners need to understand that their role is to be a 'first-aid' support to their peers by listening to them and helping them to identify solutions to a particular problem, using the active listening and decision-making skills that will be practised in the training programme. They are not there to give advice or offer solutions to the problem.

You need to explain to the peer listeners that listening actively is essential if we are to 'hear' what participants are really saying or not saying. Active listening is not just about using our ears, but often that is the only way people are listened to.

There are four levels or degrees of listening as outlined below.

### 1 Ignoring

This is the most basic and uncommitted level of listening, when we are not consciously paying attention to what is being said. We may hear some of the words but we are not processing the information contained in the sentences.

The non-verbal communication of a listener who is 'ignoring' usually gives the game away:

- very little or no eye contact;
- distracting actions such as looking out of the window or at the clock;
- continuing to do an unrelated task such as writing or picking up the phone to make a call.

---

**Why not try this?**

Ask your pupils to work in pairs and give them the following story to role-play 'ignoring listening':

Peter is being bullied by another boy who is harassing him during games,

---

taking his lunch money and also threatening to beat him up after school. Peter has not told anyone and he is afraid to tell his parents because the bully has told him that he will 'get worse' if Peter tells anyone.

Ask each member of the pair in turn to pretend to be Peter and try using the non-verbal communication points above while trying to listen. Only give them a short time, perhaps a minute, so that it does not become a chore.

After each member of the pair has completed the exercise, ask the class to comment on what it was like to be the victim trying to get their problem across, and also how it felt to be the 'ignoring listener'.

### 2 Superficial listening

This level is also known as 'going through the motions' of listening. It is probably the most frequently used level of listening.

The listener will selectively process the information being received. In other words the listener is more concerned with what their own response will be once the speaker pauses. Attention is not fully focused and only key words are heard. In this type of listening thoughts may drift elsewhere (for example, 'It's nearly lunch time, what shall we eat today?' or suddenly remembering a forgotten mobile text or call).

The non-verbal communication of the superficial listener may be more attentive than the first level but is not authentic:

- moderate eye contact (may be good, but feels like you're being looked through);
- some appropriate noises and nods of the head.

**Why not try this?**

Again, ask your pupils to try out superficial listening using the same role-play as for 'ignoring listening', or use a role-play of your own.

### 3 Content level listening

At this level the listener is actively processing all the words to make sense of the information. This is the minimum level for active listening and, depending on the situation, may be most frequently used by support workers and facilitators. In this type of listening the non-verbal communication is far more committed and authentic.

**Why not try this?**

Ask your pupils to role-play actively processing everything that they are told in the role-play.

### 4 Empathetic listening

This level is the most difficult and tiring because it requires total concentration. It is listening not only to *what* is being said (content) but also to *how* it is being said (feelings and actions). It is about being consciously aware of the speaker's tone of voice, their non-verbal communication and perhaps what they are not saying as much as what they are saying. It is important to listen at this level when dealing with any emotional or personal issue.

**Why not try this?**

Again, ask your pupils to role-play this level of listening – always remembering to keep the role-plays to a minute each time and to reverse roles.

At the end of this exercise, have a discussion about listening and what they thought. Which level was easiest? Which level made them the most uncomfortable? Do they know people (no names) who communicate on these different levels? What about television programmes that they watch – any thoughts on the level of listening required for soaps or documentaries or the news?

## Support skills

After your pupils have tried the listening exercises, ask them to think about what skills a good listener needs. The following is a list from a group of peer listeners:

- Listening attentively and respectfully.
- Thinking well about the other person.
- Being reliable.
- Showing empathy (not sympathy).
- Being non-judgemental.
- Understanding body language, tone, eye contact and facial expression.
- Starting from where the person is – not making assumptions.
- Reflecting back/checking out.
- Being non-directive (mostly).
- Using appropriate physical contact.

- Respecting confidentiality.
- Being comfortable with silence.
- Providing safety.
- Enabling the person to share feelings, experiences and fears.
- Assisting the person to express feelings.
- Accepting the person as distinct from behaviour.
- Being able to build a relationship.
- Emphasising the positive where relevant – but not shying away from despair, hopelessness, etc., if relevant.

Also ask your pupils what things might not be useful. This is the list from the same peer listeners:

- Taking over the session, bringing in your own experiences and feelings (for example, 'I know how you feel').
- Cheering someone up.
- Colluding with their despair/depression.
- Talking too much and filling the silences.
- Trivialising/giving inappropriate reactions.
- Telling people what to do, or being directive.
- Allowing people to waffle beyond a certain point.
- Making judgements.
- Offering friendship.
- Indulging in gossip.
- Not believing/laughing.

## Reflecting on practice

One school tried setting up a peer listening scheme only to find that a couple of the peer listeners took on a very unhelpful tone when pupils talked to them. One boy told a pupil that he needed to do a whole list of things to sort out the problem. The difficulty was a lack of supervision, which allowed the listeners, with the best of intentions, to become the 'know-it-alls'. This is just one of the many things to think about when setting up a peer listening scheme.

## Roadblocks to communication

Teaching pupils about communication is a big task and the attitude of the listener can easily get in the way of pupils sharing their worries. For example:

- Moralising, preaching – 'You should …'; 'You ought to …'; 'It is your responsibility …'
  - can cause a person to 'dig in' and defend their position even more (e.g. 'Who says?');
  - communicates lack of trust in a person's sense of responsibility.
- Advising, giving solutions – 'What I would do is …'; 'Why don't you …?'; 'Let me suggest …'
  - can imply that the person is not able to solve their own problems;
  - prevents a person from thinking through a problem, considering alternative solutions, and trying them out for real;
  - can cause dependency or resistance.
- Persuading with logic, arguing – 'Here is why you are wrong …'; 'The facts are …'; 'Yes, but …'
  - provokes a defensive position and counter arguments;
  - can cause the person to feel inferior and inadequate.
- Judging, criticising, blaming – 'You are not thinking maturely …'; 'You are wrong …'
  - implies incompetency, stupidity and poor judgement;
  - cuts off communication from a person over fear of negative judgement;
  - means the person sometimes accepts judgements as true ('I am bad') or retaliates ('You're not so great yourself!').
- Praising, agreeing – 'Well, I think you're doing a great job!'; 'You're right – that teacher sounds awful!'
  - implies high speaker expectations;
  - can be seen as patronising or as a manipulative effort to encourage desired behaviour;
  - can cause anxiety when the person's perception of self does not match the speaker's praise.
- Reassuring, sympathising – 'Don't worry'; 'You'll feel better'; 'Oh, cheer up'
  - causes the person to feel misunderstood;
  - evokes strong feelings of hostility ('That's easy for you to say!').
- Diverting, sarcasm – 'Let's talk about pleasant things…'
  - implies that life's difficulties are to be avoided rather than dealt with;
  - can infer that a person's problems are unimportant, petty or invalid.

## Observation and listening skills

Peer listeners need to understand that listening includes picking up clues and watching how they interact with others. Explain to your pupils that, to become skilled peer listeners, they will need to do the following:

- **Stop talking** – Give yourself the space and time to really be there with the person you are listening to.

- **Concentrate** – Focus on what is going on and don't let yourself get distracted (internally or externally). If you do, don't give yourself a hard time but return immediately to the task.

- **Watch closely** – What clues do you get from someone's face? Mouth? Hands? Eyes? And body language? Focusing on these clues will help concentration.

- **Maintain eye contact** – Keep eye contact with the person you are listening to – not a hard stare, but soft, involved eye contact, with your focus occasionally moving away.

- **Be aware of body posture** – Think about how you are sitting, how close or far away you are from the person you are listening to. Is it appropriate? Be relaxed (but alert), with your arms open and unfolded.

- **Control head and facial movements** – Show interest, respond to what the person is saying, and be natural.

- **Listen for what is *not* said** – Work out what is being left out or avoided. Trust your intuition.

- **Listen to *how* something is being said** – Don't concentrate so hard on the content that you lose out on the emotional reactions.

- **Be aware of, and try to recognise your responses and decide to put your feelings aside** – Are you switching off? Are you arguing mentally? Are you getting distracted by remembering your own experiences?

- **Recognise and be aware of your prejudices** – Try to avoid classifying and stereotyping as far as you are able.

- **Identify the main points in what is being said** – Is the person waffling? Are they trying to put you off the track?

- **Spot the value behind what is being said** – What do you think the person feels about themselves? What beliefs do they hold?

- **Look at how the person is expressing themselves** – How loudly or softly are they speaking? How quickly or slowly are they speaking? Are they using gentle or violent gestures? What mannerisms do they have?

- **Check out, check out, check out** – Have you understood accurately what the person is saying and conveying to you? If not, why not? Feel free to ask for clarification.

> ## Why not try this?
>
> Earlier in this chapter I listed the characteristics that peer supporters thought were important. If you are helping pupils become peer listeners, make sure they understand exactly what the terms mean, or ask them to come up with their own definitions of the following skills:
>
> - **Warmth and caring** – Being concerned, accepting, friendly.
> - **Empathy** – Trying to understand how it feels to be in someone else's shoes, showing that you want to understand.
> - **Non-judgemental** – Not being shocked or judging someone. Accepting the person and their feelings.
> - **Respect** – Allowing the person the right to feel any emotion and to express it.
> - **Genuineness** – Being 'real', not just playing a role.
> - **Clarifying** – Asking someone a question if you are unclear about something that has been said.
> - **Summarising** – Checking that you have understood correctly.
> - **Questioning** – Using questions that are open ended.
> - **Patience** – Waiting for the person to say everything they want.
> - **Concentration** – Focusing your mind totally on what the person is saying.

## Guidelines for effective listening

Here are some useful guidelines for effective listening:

- Relax so you can give the other person your full attention.
- Be aware of your posture – for example, lean slightly forward, adopt an open rather than closed body position, use encouraging gestures such as nods of the head.
- Use an appropriate tone of voice, pitch and volume.
- Note the speaker's tone of voice, pitch and volume – you can pick up clues on how they are feeling.
- Paraphrase and summarise what is said to you. It helps you to fully process the information and it shows the speaker that you are listening to them. But you must use your own words when doing this – don't parrot the speaker.
- Reflect back your perception of how the speaker is feeling when it is appropriate. (For example, 'You sound anxious about that', 'You seem

upset about it.') If your perception is incorrect, the speaker has a chance to respond and maybe disclose their true feelings.

- Use probing questions to gain more information and a better understanding. (For example, 'Why do think that happened?' 'How do think it will work?')

- Allow silences – people sometimes find it awkward to leave a silence and will say anything to fill it. A silence of up to 10 seconds can be used as reflection time, or getting thoughts sorted out.

## Why not try this?

Give pupils a copy of these guidelines and ask them to discuss them in small groups or with a partner. Ask them if they have any further suggestions or questions. You may want to show them how to use these guidelines in practice – for example, interview one of the pupils while you are relaxed or tense, or show body posture that is open or closed, etc.

## TOP TIPS!

*Effective listeners try to avoid:*

- *making judgements*

- *interrupting to add their own views*

- *providing solutions or answers*

- *asking leading and closed questions*

- *letting their personal feelings get in the way*

- *working out some advice to give, based on their own personal experience.*

*Effective listening is about:*

- *responding, not necessarily solving*

- *helping the other person listen to their own words and find their own solutions*

- *keeping calm and controlled.*

## Open and closed questions

Open and closed questions are an excellent tool in helping people feel comfortable and in opening up their feelings. This is the sort of exercise you may remember from teacher training. Practise it with your peer listeners – it is fun and really starts them thinking.

Pupils in distress are often vague or confused, so peer listeners may have to ask questions. But pupils also need to define their problems for themselves and not in the peer listener's terms. Good listeners avoid all but the most necessary questions. However, when helping someone to look at problems clearly and develop solutions, a key skill is the peer listener's ability to avoid closed questions and ask only those that open or stretch understanding. Some questions open up and illuminate; others close down or lead the person to the questioner's conclusions. The latter case probably marks the end of your chance to help. Questions that are open will indicate to the person being questioned that you are listening and following rather than leading them.

The table below shows the difference between open and closed questions.

| Open | Closed |
|------|--------|
| Questions that lead to the exploration of feelings and facts (for example, 'Tell me a bit more ...', 'What did it feel like ...?') | Questions that can be answered 'Yes' or 'No' |
| Questions that use *who*, *where*, *what*, *when* and *how* – helping with description rather than explanation | Questions that use *why* – usually inviting blaming, explaining, defending, justifying and placating |
| Questions that focus on one point at a time | Rhetorical questions (for example, 'Don't you think ...?') |
| Questions that neither of you know the answer to before you ask it | Questions that lead a person to 'your' answer |
| Questions that press for specific data – what precisely was said, done or felt | Questions that speculate or invite speculation (for example, 'Don't you think you'd have done better if ...?') |
| Questions that help the person to imagine a new behaviour or new self-image | |

## Why not try this?

Ask your pupils to think of how closed questions start. To what questions could you answer 'Yes' or 'No'? What words would you use to start the question? Examples might include:

- Do
- Did
- Can
- Would
- Could
- Are

What words lead to open questions, ones that you would give a full answer to and that cannot be answered by 'Yes' or 'No'? Examples might include:

- How
- When
- Where
- What
- Why

Once your pupils have come up with a list of words to start questions, ask them to work in pairs and ask closed questions. Give them one minute each to do so and then discuss how much information they got when asking 'Did you?', 'Would you?', 'Could you?', etc. Ask how many questions they had to ask to fill up the minute – it should be many, because the answers must only be 'Yes' or 'No'.

Then ask them to try the same thing asking open-ended questions, like 'What did you do on holiday?' or 'Why do you think people are worried about the environment?', etc. Again, they will each get one minute, after which you should find that they did not have to ask so many questions because the answers were fuller.

You may want to tell pupils that there are times when it is appropriate to use both kinds of questions. If you want more information, it is likely to come after an open question. A little bell should sound in your head when you start a question with 'Did you?', unless you want a 'Yes' or 'No' answer. However, it may be that you do not want a lot of information in some situations, so you may deliberately want to use closed questions.

Here are some examples of open-ended questions:

- What does that feel like?

- What would happen if you ...?
- Can you tell me more about ...?
- How are you feeling right now?
- Would you like to talk about ...?
- Where would you like to begin?
- How do you feel now about ...?
- How would you like things to be?
- What do you imagine ...?
- What have you thought of?
- What would it be like to ...?
- How do you see things changing?
- What would you like to do about ...?
- What's that like?
- What are the advantages/drawbacks of ...?
- What can you think of?
- What's most important for you now?

## Decision-making skills

Your peer listeners will also need to think about how to help pupils to make their own decisions about what to do. The peer listener is there to facilitate other pupils' thinking skills by listening and reflecting and suggesting, not telling them what they should do. Ask your peer listeners to think about what they can do to help a pupil make a decision. For example:

- Give the person space to think. Don't feel you have to get the pupil to do something immediately – they may need time.
- Check out whether you've understood them by reflecting back what they said. (For example, if a pupil says she is afraid of a group of girls, the peer listener says, 'You feel afraid.')
- Possibly point out alternatives. (For example, if the pupil says he wants to hit the bully, the peer listener might ask what else he could do, such as getting an adult involved.)
- Allow permission to make mistakes. (For example, a pupil may say he has really messed up and the peer listener may reflect that everyone has and that it is OK to make mistakes.)
- Have access to relevant and up-to-date information. Peer listeners need to know what options are available to the pupils – local help groups, websites, books and helplines.

- Offer assurance they can make the decision – reassure pupils that they have the right and power to make decisions that affect them.
- Don't make the decision for the pupil. (For example, 'Let me tell you what I would do' is *not* the way!)
- Think through the steps and be specific – help the pupil set out what they want to do. (For example, the pupil says he wants to think about things overnight, then tell his best friend, and then talk to the bully who used to be his friend; the listener helps the pupil put down the steps in his mind or on paper.)
- Think through what gets in the way of making the decision. (For example, the peer listener may ask, 'What do you think is stopping you from …?')
- Think through the consequences of the decision. (For example, ask 'If you do that, what might happen next?')
- Sort out motivations. (For example, ask 'Why do you think Harry is doing that?')
- Think about what the pupil actually wants. (For example, ask 'If this were to be the best solution, what would you want to happen?')
- Identify any support they can get for carrying out their decision. (For example, ask 'Who will help you to do that?')
- Perhaps agree time limits. (For example, ask 'How much time do you think that will take?')
- Think about how the pupil can accept other people's decisions if their own is not possible. (For example, ask 'If that doesn't work out because it is out of your hands, how can I help?')

In summary, your peer listeners can support pupils by helping them in a five-step decision-making process:

1 Identify the problem.
2 Explore the alternatives and consequences.
3 Choose the next step.
4 Act upon their choice.
5 Evaluate the results.

## Confidentiality

Peer support systems will not work if pupils think that the peer listener is going to tell or gossip about what they are told. You have to decide on the level of confidentiality that you are going to ask of your peer listeners and what you are going to tell the pupils. Both the pupils and your peer listeners also need to know when and how confidentiality may need to be broken. Who should peer listeners tell when it becomes apparent that they have been told something that is too serious to be kept to themselves? For example, if a peer listener is told that a pupil is going to harm themselves or others, or that someone is in danger, they cannot be expected to hold on to that information. Peer listeners cannot take on the kind of responsibility that an adult would – they do not have the life experience or training to act as psychologists or counsellors.

So, you could use the following as an example of what the peer listener would say in regard to confidentiality:

> I would like to reassure you that what you tell me will remain confidential. This means that I will not talk to anyone outside this room about what you tell me, in such a way that your identity would be known. Any discussion that I might have with a member of the support team will not include your name. But there could be a situation where I may have to break confidentiality – let me explain what I mean ...

The circumstances in which confidentiality will have to be broken include when:

- the peer listener's health or safety is at risk;
- another person's health or safety is at risk;
- someone is being abused;
- someone is suicidal;
- someone is using drugs;
- someone under the age of 16 is pregnant.

Talk to your peer listeners and explain that, if they need to break confidentiality, the following steps are necesssary:

- The peer listener must discuss the need to break confidentiality with the pupil, and encourage the pupil to speak to a teacher or the project coordinator, or another key member of staff. The peer listener can offer support by accompanying the pupil.
- The peer listener will need to discuss the situation with a member of staff as soon as possible – even if the pupil who told does not want to be there.
- The project coordinator will decide on the appropriate action, and who needs to be informed. The school's child protection guidelines should be referred to.
- Details of the case should be recorded (see the form at the end of this chapter) by the project coordinator. Records need to be stored in a secure location.
- The project coordinator should discuss any action taken with the pupil who disclosed the situation. At some meetings the peer listener could be present, depending upon the disclosure and the needs of the pupil.

## Supporting peer listeners

Peer supporters are usually competent, bright, altruistic and helpful pupils who may seem able to cope with most situations. But in a peer listening programme, they will all need support through meetings with other peer listeners, sessions with you as the project coordinator and opportunities to get more information and training.

Even though you may set up the peer listeners for the purpose of dealing with bullying, it is inevitable that they will be told about other things and will need adult support. You also need to give them an opportunity to offload any feelings or concerns they may have. They will need to talk about what works, what went right and what went wrong. The peer listening schemes are growth experiences for those taking part and you will want to help them debrief and to feel they are being successful. Using a pupil evaluation form can be very helpful here (see the example at the end of this chapter).

Think about giving certificates to those in the programme as a thank-you for their efforts. No matter what their ages, pupils like recognition, and perhaps having doughnuts and drinks in your training sessions will make them feel appreciated for all the extra time they are putting in.

And don't forget to appreciate yourself – how about rewarding your own efforts with a nice meal or a night out? Without you, the peer listeners would not exist.

# Conclusion

Peer support programmes can be very successful in helping to encourage pupils to talk about bullying and finding solutions. It helps to build confidence for both the peer supporters and those they help. It builds the trust between pupils and teachers and prevents and deters bullying. As one peer supporter said, 'There is a feeling of calm and positive energy in school now and we all stand up for each other instead of looking for ways to be sarcastic and nasty. I think peer supporting is the best thing that has happened to our school and to me.'

---

### Going further

**Useful websites**

www.childline.org.uk

www.kidscape.org.uk

www.mandbf.org.uk

www.teachernet.gov.uk

---

# Sample forms

## Peer listening scheme – recording form

| Date | Class/Form or year group |
|---|---|
| Ref. no. | Gender |

| Issue/Situation |
|---|
| |

| Action points |
|---|
| |

| Comments |
|---|
| |

| Peer listener |
|---|
| |

## Evaluation – pupil questionnaire

As you have just used the peer listener scheme, we would like you to help us make the scheme as useful as possible by providing the following information.

Date [          ] Year group [          ] Gender: M [  ] F [  ]

1   How did you find out about the scheme?

2   Did you see a peer listener on your own or with a friend(s)?

3   Whose idea was it to visit the scheme (yours, parent, teacher, friend)?

4   Did you see the peer listener attached to your tutor/year group?

5   How many times have you used the scheme?

6   How long (approximately) did you spend with the peer listener?

7   Please comment on how you found the scheme (friendly, helpful?).

8   Do you have any suggestions about how the scheme could be improved?

*All information given will be treated confidentially.*

# Preventative strategies
## *Michele Elliott*

**What this chapter will explore:**

- Tried and tested anti-bullying activities
- Books with anti-bullying themes

This chapter is different from others in the book because it includes 20 exercises – activities that you can delve into if you need an anti-bullying theme or lesson to use with your pupils. Because you often have too much to do and too little time to do it in, you may welcome the following ideas, which have all been used successfully with pupils. You can dip in quickly and grab an idea, which usually does not take much preparation or fancy materials. Most of the strategies and exercises can be adapted for pupils of different ages and abilities, though some are age-specific. You can also look online for lesson plans and good ideas, using sites like www.teachernet.gov.uk, www.safenetwork.org.uk and www.kidscape. org.uk, as well as many others.

# 1 Story/play

There are several books about bullying listed at the end of this chapter. You can either choose one to read or ask pupils to read a story or prepare a short play about bullying. You could ask older pupils to read to younger pupils or to put on a play for young pupils.

An example of a thought-provoking book for older pupils is *Lord of the Flies* by William Golding, which describes a group of boys who become the hunters and cast out Piggy, who is then tormented and bullied. *Whose Side Are You On?* by Alan Gibbons takes up the theme of what to do when your friend is bullied, which helps to highlight the issue of the role of bystanders in bullying. *Cuckoos* by Roger Green finds a boy and his parents bullying everyone in the entire school until the pupils start learning about cuckoos.

For younger pupils you might look at *Picking on Percy* by Cathy MacPhail, which is told with humour from Sean's viewpoint as the bully who ends up accidently swapping lives with his victim Percy. And the ever-popular Judy Blume tackles how it is easy to bully other pupils when they are different in her book *Blubber*.

You can check out the books at the end of the chapter, but you may already have some others you are familiar with and can use. If your pupils come up with plays that are good, why not post them on your website?

# 2 Collage

Collages are a fun, non-threatening way for pupils to express their feelings about bullying.

You will need magazines, which you can ask your pupils to bring in (ones with lots of pictures). You also need blank paper – A3 if possible, but A4 will do – and scissors and paste. It is also possible to make collages using computer technology, if you don't want the mess.

Ask pupils to work on a 'bullying' theme to make their collages. Tell them to go through the magazines and cut or tear out pictures that reflect the theme. Some suggestion for themes are:

● When I am bullied I feel ...

- When I see someone being bullied I ...
- People who bully are ...
- People who are bullied are ...
- What I would like to do to people who bully.
- How people who bully feel.
- How victims feel.
- What adults do about bullying.
- Bullying is ...
- People who cyberbully.
- 10 ways people bully others.
- 10 ways to stop bullying.

Display the collages, if appropriate, or ask pupils to discuss them in small groups. This exercise does not depend upon artistic talent, and pupils of all ages seem to enjoy the hands-on approach of making collages.

You can also expand the collages into more personal ways to talk with individual pupils about some issues that may arise from bullying. You might quietly ask them to put together a collage, perhaps outside school hours, which you can use as a way into talking about problems. Some themes might include:

- How I see myself.
- How others see me.
- I wish I was ...
- How my parents/teachers see me.
- How I see other pupils.

# 3 Making friends

Although we ask pupils to become friends, many have absolutely no clue about how to go about it. In fact bullying is sometimes the result of misguided attempts of pupils trying to become part of a group or trying to approach someone to become a friend.

Ask pupils to discuss ways to make friends. Working in small groups, ask them to come up with a list of 10 ways of how you can make friends. Then ask them to report to the larger group and write the suggestions on the board, avoiding duplication.

These suggestions were compiled by a group of 13-year-olds:

- Showing an interest in what other pupils do.
- Being complimentary without going over the top.
- Having a pleasant expression on your face.
- Laughing at people's jokes.
- Being kind.
- Asking others to join in.
- Offering to help.
- Inviting people to do something, like an interactive game online.
- Going to places where other pupils hang out.
- Being welcoming to new pupils.
- Bringing something interesting to do.
- Being willing to share.
- Being humorous/telling jokes.
- Being fair.
- Organising games or activities.

Using the same method, ask pupils to think about ways *not* to make friends. One group thought of the following:

- Being bossy.
- Telling others how to play.
- Telling others they are doing things wrong.
- Talking about yourself all the time.
- Bullying others online, by text or in person.
- Spreading rumours about other pupils.
- Being negative and sarcastic.
- Being too intense or serious all the time.
- Bragging.
- Moaning all the time.
- Being a bystander when someone is being bullied.
- Claiming credit for something you didn't do.
- Lying or cheating.

Ask pupils to draw up a 'friendship charter' and post it in the school where it can be seen and also on your school website. Ask pupils for feedback.

As a follow-up to 'making friends' you can also try these ideas:

- Ask pupils to role-play someone trying to make friends the wrong way and then do another role-play showing the right way.
- Ask pupils to conduct a survey asking classmates (and perhaps staff) for their ideas on making friends. Chart the results and discuss.
- Ask pupils to write a story about imaginary new pupils trying to make friends in the school – what obstacles they might encounter; what things would help? Include suggestions that the school might use to change for the better.

# 4 Letter/email to a friend

Ask pupils to write a letter or email to a pen pal (real or imaginary) or a new friend, describing what they like to do, what kind of a person they are, and what they hope to do when they leave school. In the letter, ask them to write about their life in school and to bring in the theme of bullying from the viewpoint of either a victim or a bully. For example, they can write about a typical day in school and include a bullying situation. With younger pupils you might give them a bully scenario to include if they need a little help.

# 5 Body outline

This exercise is for younger pupils. Ask each pupil to lie down on a large piece of paper (rolls of heavy lining paper from a DIY shop are perfect for this and quite cheap) and trace an outline of their bodies. Ask the pupils to cut out their outline and colour it in as they wish. Then get a pad of Post-it notes and write something good about each pupil and attach the note to the outline, perhaps on the hand. Change the message as often as possible – your pupils will be delighted and excited to see what is said about them. This can also be done on the computer.

# 6 Nicknames

Ask your pupils what nickname they would like to be called, if they had a choice. Often, hurtful nicknames are given to pupils by others and then used to bully them. You may need to help pupils find positive nicknames for themselves. This might be a good opportunity to use words from other languages, such as Solecito (Spanish for little sun), Shaina (Yiddish for beautiful), Leoncito (Spanish for little lion). Ask pupils for other suggestions. Come up with a list and let pupils decide on their own names, but don't let anyone pick a negative nickname.

You can use this to reflect on names and how they can be used for good or bad. Pupils could also make up poems or stories about names. Reflecting back on *Lord of the Flies*, what was the significance of Piggy's name?

# 7 Pupil of the week

Each week put up the picture of one pupil in your class. Ask each of the other pupils to say one good thing about the pupil and make a list of five statements to put under the picture. If you want to speed up the exercise, have a 'pupil of the day'. Try to have all the pictures and comments up on parents' evening and ask the parents to add a comment (if not all the parents can come, try to get a good comment either in writing or over the telephone and add it to the pupil's list).

Although this activity probably works best with young pupils, one secondary teacher used it very successfully with her Year 10 pupils. She said that she was surprised how eagerly her pupils looked forward to the time for their picture to be up. In a busy teaching schedule it is easy to forget how important and thrilling it is to be given a few words of praise. Some pupils may only get kind words from you, and so they remember them for many years.

# 8 Poem

Ask pupils to write a poem about bullying. Display the poems and choose some to be read at assembly or posted on your school website. Alternatively, have a contest in which judges from outside the school choose the winners, and then give the winners a book token or some other small prize (donated by a local business?).

# 9 What would you do?

Give your pupils the following case study and ask them to find solutions to this bullying problem.

**Case study**

Rhys is a good athlete and a bit full of himself. He likes being the centre of attention and is quite clever with jokes. He is not a great scholar and has some problems, especially with maths. Rhys has been bullying another boy, Archie, and many pupils are aware of it. Rhys makes sure that Archie is not allowed to play with the other boys at break or sit with them at lunch. Rhys has also been inviting others to make negative comments about Archie in chatrooms and has posted some nasty material online. Archie does well in school and has not had any previous serious bullying incidents directed at him before. He is not a bully and is increasingly distressed by what Rhys is doing. He has not told the teacher or his parents about the bullying.

- Why do you think Rhys is bullying Archie?
- What would you do if you were Archie's friend?
- What would you do if you were Rhys's friend?
- What could you do if you were a bystander?

# 10  Positive/negative

Ask pupils to draw a line down the centre of a piece of paper and write 'Positive' at the top on one side and 'Negative' on the other. Ask them to write down three positive things about themselves in the first column and three negative things in the second. The ground rule is that none of the traits can be physical (like a big nose), but should be things like character traits, attitudes or talents and therefore could be changed or modified. For example:

| Positive | Negative |
|---|---|
| Honest | Bad tempered |
| Fast runner | Doesn't do homework |
| Likes pets | Untidy |

Ask pupils to work on changing one negative trait into a positive one over the next week or month. This exercise is best done individually and not with other pupils unless a trusting relationship has been built up – otherwise the 'negatives' could be used to bully.

# 11 Class newspaper

Ask each pupil to contribute an article, drawing, puzzle or poem about bullying to a class newsletter. Have the pupils put the newsletter together and post it online, or print paper copies for parents, pupils and staff.

## Case study

Sophie was a new girl in Year 8 who came into school mid-term. To help her adjust, her teacher asked one of the mature, friendly girls, Mia, to show her around. Sophie was on edge and rebuffed any overtures made by the pupils to include her. She was perfectly pleasant to Mia but kept to herself and did not reach out. Mia continued to invite her to sit with the rest of the girls at lunch and to include her whenever she could, but Sophie resisted.

Her teacher was concerned and delved a bit into Sophie's background to see if there was any way in which she could help. Sophie had moved several times as her mother tried to get work in different towns and villages. She had no siblings and she and her mother formed a tight bond as they went through various upheavals. Talking to her teacher from her previous school, her new teacher discovered that Sophie had been bullied and excluded by a group of girls led by Sophie's so-called best friend, and that Sophie's confidence was very low. Sophie had apparently decided to protect herself by not letting anyone get close. Her teacher also found out that Sophie had a talent for writing, so she quietly called Sophie aside and said she needed a big favour. The school newspaper, which Mia worked on, needed more material, and the teacher asked if Sophie would mind writing a short piece or contributing a poem.

Sophie agreed and Mia was enthusiastic and supportive. Sophie continued to write for the paper and eventually she settled in and began to trust her fellow pupils. About three months later the pupils used the paper to start an anti-bullying campaign and Sophie wrote a fictional story about bullying based on what she had gone through.

The other pupils never found out why Sophie had been so skittish when she first arrived, but she went on to do well academically and made many friends, before she moved on again in Year 10. Sophie kept in touch with both her teacher and Mia to let them know that she had been accepted at university and was planning to become a writer. So a combination of an empathetic teacher and Mia, along with the school newspaper, helped a bullied, unhappy girl to find her feet.

# 12 Millionaire

Tell pupils that they have each inherited £1,000,000, of which they must use 90 per cent to eradicate bullying. After they have stopped all bullying, they can then use the remaining 10 per cent of the money for personal use, and they must use that 10 per cent to make their own lives happier. How would they use the money? Pupils can either work individually and write about what they would do, or work in small groups and report back to the class what they would do as a group.

# 13 Puppet play

This exercise is for younger pupils. Using socks decorated by the pupils (buttons for eyes, felt for mouths, wool for hair and whiskers) or paper cut-outs of characters, ask the pupils to make up a puppet play about a pupil who is being bullied and how sad the pupil feels. Ask them to think of a positive way to end the play so that the pupil who is bullying gets help, and so does the victim – a happy ending! You can do this with about three characters: one bully, one victim and one friend, plus a teacher puppet.

If you need to give them suggestions about a play, try the following:

- Toby was a very happy little boy.
- Leo did not like Toby and decided to bully him.
- Leo hid Toby's hat so Toby could not find it. Leo took Toby's lunch box and threw it away so Toby did not have anything to eat. Leo also said mean things about Toby
- Harry was a friend of Toby and saw what Leo did.
- Harry told Leo that it was not right to bully Toby, but Leo just laughed at him.
- Harry then told the teacher, who talked to Toby and then to Leo.
- Leo felt bad that he had hurt Toby's feelings and he apologised. The teacher asked them to shake hands and that was the end of the story.

# 14 Mural

Ask pupils to create a class mural. It should show on one panel a playground where bullying is happening and on another panel a playground where everyone is having a good time and where there is no bullying. Discuss your own playground and think of ways that could make it more like the 'no bullying' panel.

## 15 Make someone feel good

Ask pupils to agree to do or say at least one thing a day to make someone else feel good. The rule is that it has to be a different pupil each day that they approach. You may want to make this a month-long project and ask each pupil to do or say something to each member of the class or group. Ask pupils to keep a journal or record of what they do and discuss it with them.

## 16 Wish list

This exercise is best done on an individual basis and then discussed with you.

Ask pupils to write down on one side of paper five words that describe them. On the other side of the paper write down five words that they wished described them.

Ask them to take one of the words on their 'wish list' and describe what it means to be like that. For example, if they said they wished they were 'happy', what does it mean to them to be happy? They might say that people who seem to be happy:

- smile
- have friends
- do well in school
- have money
- come from nice families
- feel good about themselves.

Then ask your pupil to look at the list they have just made to see which things it might be possible for them to work on to become happy. It might not be possible to have money (or necessarily even true that you need it to be happy) or to come from a nice family, but it might be possible to work on smiling, having friends, doing well in school and feeling good about themselves.

Ask pupils to make it a goal to work on attaining at least one of the ideals on their wish list. Help them work out an action plan to achieve their goal. For example, if the goal is to 'be popular', then the pupil needs to think about how they can make friends and show welcoming and friendly behaviour (see 'Making friends' above). Their action plan might start something like this:

- Try to smile at people whenever possible.
- Be kind to other pupils and offer to help.
- Invite another pupil home.
- Be ready to listen to others.

For 'doing well in school', the action plan might look like this:

- Start by choosing one subject to work on.
- Ask your teacher for extra help.
- Set aside more time to work on that subject.
- Study with someone who might be able to help you understand it better.
- Don't get discouraged if it takes some time to improve in the subject.
- Tell yourself that you will improve – and believe that you can do it.
- Ignore anyone who attempts to discourage you, even a well-meaning parent who says, 'I never did very well in that either.'
- Reward yourself for getting better.

This exercise helps people to develop self-esteem if they follow through and actually are able to change the goal from a wish to a reality. Although it does take lots of help and encouragement, it is worth it to achieve the goal. Pupils can do this exercise with parents and other adults, if they are supportive. As a teacher, you can also suggest it, but the time it takes may be too great given your other tasks.

# 17 Bully group

Ask pupils to write a story about someone who suddenly finds that they are being pulled into a group of bullies and being pressured to start bullying a person they have been friends with in the past. Part of the pressure is to contribute to a hate website and to text the pupil being bullied.

Ask your pupils to write about what the character who is resisting this pressure might be thinking and feeling and how they resolve the problem. Use the pupils' stories as a springboard to discuss how hard it is to resist peer pressure and how many people who bully others might not really want to bully but are frightened or led into this type of behaviour. How can they get help to stop? If you have a pupil newspaper, you could publish the best stories.

Once the pupils have completed this exercise, as a follow-up you can ask them to write the same story from the viewpoint of the victim. Victims will be confused, frightened and worried, especially if one of their friends joins the bullies. You can follow this with discussion about how the victims of bullying feel and how they can get help.

## 18 Bulletin board

Over the period of one month, ask pupils to look for references to bullying in the press, including racist attacks or attacks on gay or lesbian people, or incidents of suicide or suicide attempts attributed to bullying. Use these stories to create a bulletin board, either in your classroom or online. Discuss how using terms like 'gay' to bully has become widespread, and ask if they know why. Being called gay can be viewed as an insult when pupils are uncomfortable with issues of sexuality, especially with homosexuality (for ideas about dealing with these issues in more depth, see www.stonewall. org.uk and www.eachaction.org.uk). See also www.equalhumanrights.com.

## 19 Mystery person

Give each pupil the name of another pupil and tell them to keep the name of their person a secret. Ask them to contact their mystery person in confidence to find out all sorts of facts about them – not just biographical details, but names of their pets, the kinds of food they like, their secret ambitions, etc. Ask the pupils to write about their mystery person without giving their name, and then ask them to read aloud their writing to see if the class can guess who the person is. Start with general information like:

- My mystery person loves chocolate ice cream and Chinese food (not mixed together). My mystery person secretly wants to become a famous rock star and dye their hair blue.
- My mystery person likes to go swimming in the holidays. They nearly got run over by a car when they were 3 years old.
- My mystery person likes to draw, make models of ships and take things apart to see how they work.
- My mystery person is known to smile often.
- My mystery person has two brothers, a cat, a dog and a gerbil. They like the pets, but sometimes can't stand their brothers.
- My mystery person has brown hair and brown eyes and is 145 cm tall. Who are they?

At various points before the end of the reading, ask pupils to raise their hands if they think they know who the mystery person is. The comments being read out should all be positive (you may wish to check the stories) and gradually get more specific, so that the identity of the mystery person becomes apparent. This is a good way to focus positively on a pupil, making them the centre of attention in a nice way and revealing new information which might be interesting and enhance their standing with other pupils.

**TOP TIP!**

*If you are having severe bullying problems with your pupils, skip this exercise. It could become quite negative if bullies try to use it detrimentally.*

## 20 Letter/email to a bully

Ask pupils to write a letter to an imaginary bully to try to explain why they should try to change, and give some suggestions on how to change.

Alternatively, ask your pupils to write to an imaginary victim of bullying, telling the victim how they will personally help them to stop being a victim and giving advice about how the victim might get some help.

## Conclusion

Some of these exercises could be adapted for assemblies or plays (also see Chapters 6 and 7). Schools that have successfully combated bullying find that the more time they devote to keeping bullying on the agenda, the fewer incidents of bullying are reported. So the time spent on exercises like these, which promote good citizenship, actually save time in the end.

**Going further**

**Useful websites**

www.eachaction.org.uk

www.equalhumanrights.com

www.kidscape.org.uk

www.safenetwork.org.uk

www.stonewall.org.uk

www.teachernet.gov.uk

**Books for 5–7 year-olds**

Browne, A., *Willy the Champ* (Walker Books, 2008).

Browne, A., *Willy the Wimp* (Walker Books, 2008).

Cave, K., *Something Else* (Puffin, 1995).

Duran, A., *Big Bad Bunny* (Orchard, 2000).

Green, J., *I Feel Bullied* (Wayland, 1999).

Grindley, S., *Feather Wars* (Bloomsbury, 2003).

Impey, R., *Trouble with the Tucker Twins* (Puffin, 1993).

MacPhail, C., *Picking on Percy* (Barrington Stoke, 2006).

Wilson, J., *Monster Eyeballs* (Egmont Books, 2002).

**Books for 8–11 year-olds**

Alexander, L., *Hope and the Bullies* (Young Voice, 2004).

Amos, J., *Bully* (Cherrytree Books, 2006).

Blackman, M., *Cloud Busting* (Yearling, 2005).

Blume, J., *Blubber* (Macmillan, 2006).

Chambers, A., *The Present Takers* (Red Fox, 1994).

Elliott, M., *Willow Street Kids Beat the Bullies* (Macmillan, 1997).

Fine, A., *The Angel of Nitshill Road* (Egmont Books, 2007).

Gibbons, A., *Chicken* (Orion, 1994).

Ironside, V., *The Huge Bag of Worries* (Hodder, 2004).

Johnson, P., *Avenger* (Yearling, 2004).

Rowling, J., *Harry Potter and the Philosopher's Stone* (Bloomsbury, 1997).

Singer, N., *Feather Boy* (HarperCollins, 2002).

Wilson, J., *Bad Girls* (Yearling, 2006).

**Books for 12–16 year-olds**

Brugman, A., *Walking Naked* (Faber & Faber, 2004).

Coppard, Y., *Bully* (Red Fox, 1991).

Dicamillo, K., *Tiger Rising* (Walker Books, 2002).

Elliott, M., *Bullying Wise Guide* (Hodder, 2005).

Forde, C., *Fat Boy Swim* (Egmont Books, 2003).

Gardner, G., *Inventing Elliott* (Orion, 2004).

Gary, K., *Malarkey* (Red Fox, 2003).

Gibbons, A., *Whose Side Are You On?* (Orion, 1994).

Golding, W., *Lord of the Flies* (Faber & Faber, 1954).

Green, R., *Cuckoos* (Oxford University Press, 1998).

Johnson, P., *Traitor* (Yearling, 2002).

MacPhail, C., *Run Zan Run* (Bloomsbury, 2005).

McKay, H., *Indigo's Star* (Hodder, 2004).

# A whole-school approach
## *Michele Elliott*

**What this chapter will explore:**

- Finding out the extent of bullying
- Agreeing rules or guidelines
- Setting up an effective anti-bullying policy
- Implementing the anti-bullying policy

Bullying makes life more difficult for teachers. Dealing with the aftermath of a bullying case means you have to talk to the bully and victim, and perhaps the parents. Then you have to be alert for the revenge that may follow. In a day fraught with demands on your time, bullying is just one of a thousand things. No wonder it goes on.

Life would be so much easier for everyone in schools if there was less bullying. But with a little bit of effort, it is possible to reduce bullying substantially. In fact, by spending just a few hours dealing with the problem at the start of the school year, school staff could save hundreds of hours of aggravation later.

The most effective way to deal with bullying is to have a whole-school programme and policy. The law requires schools to have an anti-bullying policy, but it is the whole-school approach, including the policy, that makes the difference. The initiative for this can come from staff or parents. Once a whole-school policy is in place, it is more difficult for bullying to go on, as the combined force of the school and community will ensure that it is simply not tolerated – in any way, shape or form.

# Finding out the extent of bullying

When setting up a whole-school policy, it is a good idea first to find out the extent of the problem in the school.

> ## Why not try this?
>
> Ask pupils to fill out an anonymous questionnaire about bullying. Either make up your own questionnaire or use the models at the end of this chapter. This information will give you an indication of what is happening. Although some schools ask for the names of those who bully, this could affect the veracity of the pupils and invite abuse. ('If I find out anyone's put down my name, I'll thump them.') What you are trying to find out in the survey is if the pupils find bullying a problem, and when, where and how bullying is happening. If you compile your own survey, it should not take long to put all the results together. Otherwise, you could ask a trusted parent-volunteer to collate the results.

Once you have the results of your survey, next call a meeting with staff to share these results and discuss the implications of the survey. Decide on how to share with pupils, or perhaps invite the pupils to present the results. A whole-school assembly takes less time, but smaller classroom discussions bring out more information.

# Agreeing rules or guidelines

The next step in setting up a whole-school programme is to agree rules or guidelines.

## Class rules or guidelines

Each class can put together five or ten 'rules' they would ideally like everyone to live by in the school. (Some teachers say they prefer the term 'guidelines' – but it does not really matter what you call them as long as you all agree.) This can be a group or individual assignment. You may wish to extend these rules beyond bullying. To protect those pupils who are shy or may be victimised, you could invite pupils to comment on or suggest rules online.

## School rules or guidelines

With the pupils (and perhaps the student council if you have one) you can then put together a list of rules, using the class rules as a guideline. Limit the number of rules so that you don't end up with a manifesto that is impossible to live by (one group of pupils compiled a list that would have done the Spanish Inquisition proud!).

## Staff approval

Either ask teachers who were instrumental in leading the idea of rules to present the list to the staff, or invite pupils to do so. Or you could have a combination of both. The problem, of course, with a combined meeting is time and also sometimes the resistance of staff. However, a combined meeting helps to establish a more solid pupil–teacher response to bullying.

## Pupil vote

If you have plenty of time, you can also organise a vote by the pupils, although you don't want this to become overly complicated. Some schools have used pupil voting as a lesson in democracy, with speeches and discussion. If the staff have decided to change dramatically the original proposals it would be counter-productive to exclude the pupils at this stage. But you could skip this stage if there are no or few changes. Make the ballot secret if you have a real problem with bullying. If not, a school assembly with a show of hands speeds up the process.

## Displaying rules

You can display the school rules online or in poster form in classrooms, corridors, the lunchroom and playgrounds, so that everyone can see them. Remember that these rules might include things besides anti-bullying statements.

## School contract

From the rules that are agreed, draw up a common contract (see the example at the end of this chapter) which will be signed by each pupil. The contract works best if also signed by the parents, so that no one can later say, 'I didn't know anything about the rules!' The contract could be printed on coloured paper, funds permitting, and kept in each pupil's file. However, although school contracts are being used in many schools, there is some controversy about their legality, so you will need to ask your local authority about this.

## Support of school governors

Depending upon your school, gaining the support of the school governors may be the first stage in the whole process. Most governors, however, will be able to make a more informed decision with the survey results and the proposed rules. Otherwise, you may spend time debating the issues and then have to call another meeting.

## Support of parents

By now some of the parents will have heard something about bullying. You may want to send a letter home at an early stage to say you are looking into the problem. This could lead to thousands of emails and telephone calls from parents anxious to tell you about their child's problem, or from parents of bullies calling to ask if you are starting a vendetta against their child. If you want to send a preliminary letter home, there is an example at the end of this chapter.

One school just sent home a letter saying that the rules had been agreed and asked concerned parents to get in touch. They only had six calls in a school of 180 pupils, so this would seem to be the most time-efficient method, depending upon the verbosity of your parents. Parents are usually only too pleased that the school is taking the initiative and most parents sign the contract and agree to the rules with no problem.

**TOP TIP!**

*Calling a meeting for parents at the beginning of the year to set out your rules and anti-bullying policy shows that you take bullying seriously. This would be a good opportunity to ask pupils to present a short play, story or poem about bullying.*

### Involving the local authority

You may want to check with your local authority to see if they have any guidelines about setting school rules. They may even have already sent you some! If not, they may use your efforts as a model for other schools. Alternatively, the local authority may have suggestions from other schools or from their policy department that may be useful to you.

# Setting up an effective anti-bullying policy

Having agreed your school rules, you may want to include them in your school's anti-bullying policy. By law every school must have an anti-bullying policy, so you should already have at least a basic policy, even if it needs updating. If you would like an example of an anti-bullying policy, go online to www.kidscape.org.uk where you can download the Kidscape anti-bullying policy. Briefly, an anti-bullying policy should include the following:

- A statement of intent – that bullying of any kind is unacceptable.
- A definition of bullying – following the example in Chapter 1.
- A statement about why it is important to respond to bullying.
- The objectives of the policy – for example, that all staff, pupils and parents need to understand how to report bullying.
- Signs and symptoms of bullying – as listed in Chapter 1.
- The procedure for reporting bullying.
- Outcomes/sanctions – what will happen if bullying is uncovered and proven.
- Ways of prevention – the school rules you have agreed.
- Sources of help – organisations from which pupils, parents and teachers can get additional advice and information.

**Reflecting on practice**

Hopefully you are in a school that has developed and implemented an effective anti-bullying policy covering all the areas listed above and maybe more. But all this work is only as good as the will to follow through and ensure that the policy is used. Check if your policy:

● is easily accessible to staff, pupils and parents, both online and in written form;

● has clear guidelines about sanctions;

● sets out how to report bullying confidentially if necessary, either in person or online;

● has ever been used;

● has been looked at on at least a yearly basis.

An anti-bullying policy does not have to be long and complicated – just straightforward and in plain English. It is how it is used that makes the difference.

# Implementing the anti-bullying policy

How do you continue to implement your anti-bullying policy?

## School assemblies

During school assemblies, remind the pupils that yours is a 'telling' school and that everyone has the responsibility to tell if they see bullying happening. If the pupils are still worried about reporting bullying, make sure there is a secure way for them to do this online or in person.

**TOP TIP!**

*With younger pupils you can install a box where they can put in notes. The notes can include suggestions about homework, lunches, school journeys and other issues, as well as about bullying.*

## Supervision

Teachers cannot be in all places at all times. Bullying can happen online, out of the reach of teachers, or in school when there is no supervision, or when the supervisors are untrained, but willing, volunteers. To decrease the possibility of bullying, invite supervisors to the meetings on bullying, and make sure that they know the rules and have a clear idea of what to do and who to tell if something happens. If you are unfortunate enough to occupy one of those buildings designed to enhance bullying, then rotate pupil monitors, get in parent-volunteers, vary movement of classes by a few minutes if possible, and look at those hidden places that encourage bullying. Structure the playground time with games or activities and include quiet areas. Ask all the staff to keep a friendly eye on things as they pass by groups of pupils and places of known difficulty.

## School bus drivers

Remember to find out how much training your school bus drivers have had about dealing with bullying. Earlier I mentioned Ben (11), who was bullied at school and on the school bus. The driver joined in what he later said he thought was teasing, but it *was* bullying. It left Ben without any adult protection on those journeys. Sadly it became too much and he hanged himself, though he probably meant only to cry for help. Since bullying on the school bus is reported by many pupils as a problem, it is vital that drivers know what they should do, which is to:

- forbid bullying
- never join in
- tell the staff about any incidents.

One major difficulty is that drivers are often alone and in charge of 40 or 50 pupils. This is a recipe for disaster. How can we expect one person to drive and supervise that many pupils?

Kidscape now offers training for school bus drivers, having been in contact with Ben's family. See www.kidscape.org.uk for a general leaflet for pupils about safety issues when taking the bus.

### Why not try this?

Have a poster contest and award prizes to those who best capture the ways to deal with bullies. Ask a local business to give prizes and invite the local media to cover the story. Be sure to suggest that the pupils make up posters about all kinds of bullying, including cyberbullying. You might need to set a few guidelines, since in one school a poster from a 10-year-old showed a bully being hanged – not good. Ask the pupils to create only positive posters.

## Curriculum

Sometimes pupils do what a bully tells them because they are frightened or just don't know what to do. You can help pupils with strategies by introducing programmes in school that deal with bullying.

For example:

- See www.kidscape.org.uk for specific programmes for the age group you teach.
- Use the books listed by age appropriateness at the end of Chapter 12 as a starting point for lessons.
- Use the examples of 'What if?' questions at the end of this chapter for discussion.
- For older pupils, give them a scenario and ask them to make up their own role-plays.

Any work that it is possible to squeeze into the curriculum on self-esteem and assertiveness also helps. Good staff–pupil relationships are vital in helping pupils to develop self-esteem, which in turn helps prevent them from becoming both bullies and victims.

## Transition

Ragging and initiation rites of passage have institutionalised bullying in many schools in the past. Hopefully, these practices have been stamped out, but pupils do still fear the transition periods from primary to secondary school. If you ask any group of pupils about to enter secondary school, you will find that many are worried that they might be bullied or picked on when they arrive. Most good teachers are aware of pupils' concerns about this transition period. Pupils are invited to spend a morning in their new school and questions and worries are addressed. Perhaps you could go one step further, as some schools have done, and assign the new pupils an older pupil to show them around and ease the way. Since much bullying comes from slightly older pupils, this might also help to change the attitude of the older pupils to one of protection instead of harassment.

## Intervention

The attitude of 'Let the kids sort it out themselves' plays right into the hands of the bullies. It allows them unfettered power. When bullying is identified, immediate intervention is crucial. In fact it is a good statement to have in your anti-bullying policy. This gives a clear message that bullying of any kind will not be tolerated and that action will be taken. After the initial action, it is also important to consider help for the bully and victim (see Chapters 8 and 9). If it is a serious bullying situation, the parents should be informed and the bully may face suspension or even exclusion.

## Consequences

Your anti-bullying policy should deal with consequences meted out to those who break the rules. If these are clearly spelt out in the policy, it lessens the hassle when you have to enforce the rules. These consequences can be posted online, along with the rules, or explained to pupils in class or in assembly.

---

### Why not try this?

The only effective way to break up groups of bullies is to meet with the bullies separately and break down the group identity and ethos that encourage bullying. The following suggestions for dealing with groups come from various teachers and staff members:

- Meet with victim or victims separately and ask them to write down what happened.
- Meet with each member of the group separately and ask them to write down what happened.
- Agree with each member of the group separately what you expect and discuss how they have broken their contract.
- Meet with the group and ask each pupil to state what happened in your individual meeting; ensure that everyone is clear about what everyone else has said. This eliminates the later comment, 'I really fooled him', since everyone has admitted their part in front of the group.
- Prepare them to face their peer group: 'What are you going to say when you leave here?'
- Whatever is decided, reiterate to all pupils that they are all responsible if anyone is being bullied – there are no innocent bystanders.
- Talk to parents of all involved – show them the written statements.
- Keep a file on bullying, with all statements and penalties.
- Teach victim strategies (see Chapter 8).
- Do not accept false excuses (see Chapter 7):
  - If the bullying was an accident, did the pupils act by helping the victim or getting help or giving sympathy?
  - If it was just for a laugh, was everyone laughing?
  - If it was a game, was everyone enjoying it?

---

- If a pupil is injured, ask the parents to take photographs of the injury.
- If groups of bullies from outside your school appear, take photographs — they tend to run when they see a camera.
- If there is serious injury, contact the police.

## Conclusion

By setting up a whole-school approach to eliminating bullying, you are sending signals to the pupils that you do care about their welfare. This approach assumes good pupil–staff relations and creates an atmosphere that continues to foster those relationships. Involving parents and the community will help to change attitudes that encourage bullying. Remember, the ultimate goal of all teachers is to make bullying unthinkable.

## Sample documents

### Questionnaires

These questionnaires are examples that you can use to find out the extent of bullying in your school. You can use them as they are or give them to your pupils to help them come up with their own. The questionnaires can be put online or you could print them off. With younger pupils you may want to read out the questions.

Tick boxes are easiest to use and pupils will not feel you can tell who they are by their handwriting. For very young children you can use smiley and frowny faces.

### Questionnaire for primary/junior pupils

1   Are you being bullied?
    Yes ☐   No ☐

2   Do you know anyone being bullied?
    Yes ☐   No ☐

3   Where is the bullying?
    PE ☐   Lunchroom ☐
    School bus ☐   Hall ☐

Classroom ☐   On mobile ☐

Online ☐

4   Did you tell?

Yes ☐   No ☐

5   If you told, who did you tell?

Mum ☐   Dad ☐

Teacher ☐   Friend ☐

Gran ☐   Sister ☐

Brother ☐   Other ☐

6   Did the bullying stop?

Yes ☐   No ☐

7   Is the bully a:

Girl ☐   Boy ☐   Both ☐

**Questionnaire for older pupils**

1   Have ever been bullied?

Yes ☐   No ☐

2   At what age?

Under five ☐   5–11 ☐   11–14 ☐   Over 14 ☐

3   When was the last time you were bullied?

Today ☐   Within the last month ☐   Within the last six months ☐

A year or more ago ☐

4   Were you bullied:

Once ☐   Several times ☐   Almost every day ☐

Several times a day ☐

5   Where were you bullied?

At home ☐   Going to or from school ☐   In the playground ☐

At lunch ☐  In the toilets ☐  On the school bus ☐

In the classroom ☐  By text ☐  Online ☐  Other ☐

6   Did/do you consider the bullying to have been:

No problem ☐  Worrying ☐  Frightening ☐

So bad that you didn't want to go out or to school ☐

7   Did the bullying:

Have no effects ☐  Some bad effects ☐  Terrible effects ☐

Make you change your life in some way (e.g. change schools or move out of a neighbourhood) ☐

8   What do you think of bullies?

No feeling ☐  Feel sorry for them ☐  Dislike them ☐

Like them ☐

9   Who is responsible when bullying continues to go on?

The bully ☐  The bully's parents ☐  The teachers ☐

The headteacher ☐  The victim ☐

Bystander pupils who are not being bullied but do not help the victim ☐

Others ☐

10  Please tick if you are a:

Girl ☐  Boy ☐

11  Was the bully (bullies) a:

Girl ☐  Boy ☐  Both ☐

12  If you have ever been bullied, was the bullying:

Physical ☐  Emotional ☐  Verbal ☐  By email ☐  Online ☐

In a game ☐  In a text ☐  Photographs on mobile ☐

Other cyber ☐  Homophobic ☐  Racist ☐

(you may tick more than one)

13  Have you ever bullied anyone?

Yes ☐   No ☐

14  Have you even known someone was being bullied and did not help?

Yes ☐   No ☐

15  Where did the bullying happen?

Classroom ☐   Gym ☐   Playground ☐   Library ☐   Lunchroom ☐

Hall ☐   Stairs ☐   Bus ☐   Online ☐   Other ☐

16  When did it happen?

Morning ☐   Afternoon ☐   On the way to or from school ☐

Other ☐

17  Did you tell anyone?

Yes ☐   No ☐

18  If you did tell, who did you tell?

Friend ☐   Teacher ☐   Member of staff ☐   Parents ☐   Other ☐

19  Has the bullying stopped?

Yes ☐   No ☐

If you would like to add anything, please do so here: _____

_____

_____

## Contract example

This is a school contract that was drawn up by Year 6 pupils. Their teachers approved – would you?

1   We will not tolerate bullying or harassing of any kind.
2   We will be tolerant of others, regardless of race, religion, culture or disabilities.
3   We will not pass by if we see anyone being bullied – we will either try to stop the bullying or go for help.
4   We will not allow bullying on the way to or from school, either on the school bus or public transport, or walking.

5   We will allow a quiet area in the playground for those who do not want to run around or take part in games.

6   We will use our 'time-out room' if we feel angry, or under pressure, or just need time to calm down or work out what is wrong.

7   We will not litter or draw on school property (walls, toilets, books, etc.).

8   We will be kind to others, even if they are not our friends, and we will make new pupils feel welcome.

9   On school journeys we will act in a way that brings credit to our school.

10   We will have a discussion group once a week in class to talk about any problems that are bothering us.

11   We will be honest when asked about anything that we have done or are supposed to have done.

12   We will tell if we know about anyone being bullied by text or email or online.

## Letter to parents

This letter can be sent to parents, to let them know that you are addressing the problem of bullying.

*Dear*

*There has been much national media attention recently about the problem of bullying. As far as we are aware, our school does not have a particular problem with bullying, but we would like to ensure that this is the case. We know that pupils learn better when they are happy and not worried.*

*Having talked with the pupils, we have decided that an anonymous survey about bullying might be helpful. We will be giving the pupils the enclosed questionnaire and thought that you would like to see a copy. We will obviously keep you informed of the results, and we value your support.*

*We are giving the pupils the survey on [date]. If you have any questions, there will be a brief meeting for parents on [date]. If you could keep any questions until this meeting, we would greatly appreciate it, as we are so busy at the moment with the start of the school year.*

*Thank you for your support.*

*Yours sincerely*

## What if? questions

These questions are useful starting points to open up the issue of bullying. They can be used verbally, in writing or online, and either with individual pupils or as discussion points in small groups.

The suggested answers here are for discussion only – your pupils may have ideas that will work just as well or better.

1   You are walking to school and a gang of older bullies demands your money. Do you:

   a) fight them

   b) shout and run away

   c) give them the money?

   *a) Give them the money – your safety is more important than the money.*

2   You are in the school playground and someone accidentally trips you. Do you:

   a) hit the person hard

   b) give them a chance to apologise

   c) sit down and cry?

   *b) Give the person a chance. If it was an accident, then they should say sorry.*

3   You are in the school toilet and an older pupil comes in, punches you, and then tells you not to do anything or 'You'll get worse'. You know who the person is and you have never done anything to them. Do you:

   a) wait until the person leaves and then tell a teacher

   b) get in a fight with the person

   c) accept what happened and don't tell?

   *a) You didn't deserve to be punched and the bully was wrong to do it. If you don't tell, the bully will just keep on beating up other pupils.*

4   You are walking into the lunchroom and someone yells out a negative comment directed at you. Do you:

   a) ignore it

   b) yell back

   c) tell?

   *a) You can either ignore it (if it is the first time and that's all that happens) or c) tell if it really bothers you. People should not yell out negative comments at you.*

5   You are continually harassed by bullies calling you names, making rude comments about your mother and generally making you miserable. Do you:

a) tell them to back off

b) get a group together and make comments back

c) if possible, get a witness and then tell

d) just live with it because it isn't really bullying?

c) *Name-calling that makes you miserable is bullying and should not go on. Tell, even if you don't have a witness.*

6   You see someone you hardly know being picked on by a bully. Do you:

a) walk by and be thankful it isn't you

b) immediately rush to the defence of the victim and push the bully away

c) get help from other pupils

d) tell someone on the staff?

c) *If possible, solve the problem with other pupils, but be careful not to fight the bully. Then tell what happened.*

7   You are walking in your neighbourhood on a Saturday morning. Someone you know from school comes by you, pushes you and grabs your money before running off. Do you:

a) tell your parents

b) tell your teacher

c) tell the police

d) chase after the person?

c) *The person has committed a crime. You will also need to tell your parents. Be wary of chasing the person – you could be hurt and possessions are not worth your safety. As for the school, this has nothing to do with it as it happened away from the school grounds. You may wish your teacher to know, but it is not their responsibility to do anything about it.*

8  You know that a friend of yours is bullying someone by sending texts and putting nasty messages on a website. Do you:
   a) keep quiet so you won't be bullied by the bully
   b) tell your friend to stop it
   c) tell another friend
   d) tell your parents or teacher

   d) *This is the sensible thing to do, unless you think that your friend likes you enough to stop if you ask. If you keep quiet you are just as bad as the bully.*

9  Your teacher, bus driver or a staff member bullies you. Do you:
   a) tell your parents
   b) talk to the teacher
   c) tell the headteacher
   d) put up with it?

   a) *It is best to start with your parents, though it will be necessary to tell the headteacher. Talk with the teacher if you think they don't realise it is bothering you, but whatever you do don't put up with it.*

10  Your father (mother) bullies you. Do you:
   a) tell your teacher
   b) tell a favourite aunt (gran, uncle, etc.)
   c) do nothing as telling might make it worse?

   b) *If you have a relative to confide in, start there. Perhaps your other parent could help. Doing nothing is one way out, but it won't stop the bullying.*

# Resources and further reading

## Advice and support

### Anti-bullying charities

Anti-Bullying Network: www.antibullying.net
*Anti-bullying support for schools and research into bullying.*

Bullying UK: www.bullying.co.uk
*Advice for children, young people and parents, on its website and by email.*

Kidscape: www.kidscape.org.uk
*Leading UK charity for the prevention of bullying: free courses for bullied pupils (ZAP), peer mentoring and anti-bullying training for teachers, a helpline for parents, plus books, leaflets and DVDs.*

### Counselling/listening

ChildLine: www.childline.org.uk
*24-hour freephone helpline for children and young people on any issue, including bullying.*

National Society for the Prevention of Cruelty to Children (NSPCC): www.nspcc.org.uk
*Helpline and advice about preventing cruelty to children.*

Samaritans: www.samaritans.org
*24-hour helpline for anyone with problems.*

Youth Access: www.youthaccess.org.uk
*Information about where to find local counsellors for young people.*

## Home education

Education Otherwise: www.education-otherwise.org
*Support for families whose children are being educated outside school.*

## Homophobic bullying

EACH: www.eachaction.org.uk
*Help for adults and young people affected by homophobia or transphobia, including a freephone helpline.*

Stonewall: www.stonewall.org.uk
*Information and advice about tackling bullying of lesbian, gay and bisexual pupils.*

## Internet safety

Childnet International: www.childnet-int.org
*Information for children, teachers and parents about how to make the internet safer.*

## Legal advice

Advisory Centre For Education (ACE): www.ace-ed.org.uk
*Free advice for parents and publications for parents and professionals about a wide range of school-based issues.*

Children's Legal Centre: www.childrenslegalcentre.com
*Advice from lawyers and professionals with experience in child law, including specific information about bullying and the law.*

Education Law Association (ELAS): www.educationlawassociation.org.uk
*Directs people to legal educational professionals who may be able to help them with education law.*

Scottish Child Law Centre: www.sclc.org.uk
*Free legal advice about children and Scottish law.*

## Parents

Directgov: www.direct.gov.uk
*Advice for parents about bullying.*

Education.com: www.education.com
*US-based website with advice and reference articles about bullying.*

Kidscape: www.kidscape.org.uk
*Helpline and advice for parents about preventing bullying.*

Parentline Plus: www.parentlineplus.org.uk
*Advice from trained parent helpers about parenting issues of any kind.*

## Peer support

Kidscape: www.kidscape.org.uk
*Peer support training for schools.*

Mentoring and Befriending Foundation: www.mandbf.org.uk
*Support and guidance for organisations involved in mentoring.*

## Playground design advice

Learning Through Landscapes: www.ltl.org.uk
*Information, books and advice on improving playgrounds and outdoor spaces.*

## Racial bullying

Equal Human Rights: www.equalhumanrights.com
*Information on a wide variety of subjects, such as lesson plans for teachers, aimed at tackling racism.*

## School phobia

Phobic Awareness: www.phobic-awareness.org
*Programmes, books and information about school and other phobias.*

## Statistics

Office of National Statistics: www.ons.gov.uk
*Information about the UK's economy and society.*

## Teacher sites

Association of Teachers and Lecturers: www.atl.org.uk
*Education union giving advice about bullying for teachers.*

TeacherNet: www.teachernet.gov.uk
*Advice to teachers about bullying.*

## Voluntary standards

Safe Network: www.safenetwork.org.uk
*Advice through its website to build common standards for voluntary and community organisations.*

## Web protection

Conduct: www.schoolbehaviour.co.uk
*Software company providing web-based application for teachers to record, monitor and analyse the behaviour of pupils.*

Teachers2Parents: www.teachers2parents.co.uk
*Fully managed web-based program for communicating with parents.*

# Books with themes of bullying, friendship and safety

## Books for 3–5 year-olds

Damjan, M., *Big Squirrel and Little Rhinoceros* (Pavilion, 2009).

Dodd, L., *Scarface Claw* (Puffin, 2009).

Elliott, M., *Feeling Happy, Feeling Safe* (Hodder, 1991).

Jennings, L., *Fred* (Little Tiger Press, 1996).

McCaferty, J. and Roxbee Cox, P., *Don't Be A Bully, Billy* (Usborne, 2004).

Rosen, M., *Little Rabbit Foo Foo* (Walker Books, 2003).

Ross, T., *Is It Because?* (Andersen Press, 2006).

Simon, F., *Hugo and the Bully Frogs* (Gullane Children's Books, 2005).

Thomas, J., *Can I Play?* (Egmont Books, 2003).

Van Genechten, G., *Flop-Ear and His Friends* (Cat's Whiskers, 2005).

## Books for 5–7 year-olds

Browne, A., *Willy the Champ* (Walker Books, 2008).

Browne, A., *Willy the Wimp* (Walker Books, 2008).

Cave, K., *Something Else* (Puffin, 1995).

Duran, A., *Big Bad Bunny* (Orchard, 2000).

Green, J., *I Feel Bullied* (Wayland, 1999).

Grindley, S., *Feather Wars* (Bloomsbury, 2003).

Impey, R., *Trouble with the Tucker Twins* (Puffin, 1993).

MacPhail, C., *Picking on Percy* (Barrington Stoke, 2006).

Wilson, J., *Monster Eyeballs* (Egmont Books, 2002).

## Books for 8–11 year-olds

Alexander, L., *Hope and the Bullies* (Young Voice, 2004).

Amos, J., *Bully* (Cherrytree Books, 2006).

Blackman, M., *Cloud Busting* (Yearling, 2005).

Blume, J., *Blubber* (Macmillan, 2006).

Chambers, A., *The Present Takers* (Red Fox, 1994).

Elliott, M., *Willow Street Kids Beat the Bullies* (Macmillan, 1997).

Fine, A., *The Angel of Nitshill Road* (Egmont Books, 2007).

Gibbons, A., *Chicken* (Orion, 1994).

Ironside, V., *The Huge Bag of Worries* (Hodder, 2004).

Johnson, P., *Avenger* (Yearling, 2004).

Rowling, J., *Harry Potter and the Philosopher's Stone* (Bloomsbury, 1997).

Singer, N., *Feather Boy* (HarperCollins, 2002).

Wilson, J., *Bad Girls* (Yearling, 2006).

## Books for 12–16 year-olds

Brugman, A., *Walking Naked* (Faber & Faber, 2004).

Coppard, Y., *Bully* (Red Fox, 1991).

Dicamillo, K., *Tiger Rising* (Walker Books, 2002).

Elliott, M., *Bullying Wise Guide* (Hodder, 2005).

Forde, C., *Fat Boy Swim* (Egmont Books, 2003).

Gardner, G., *Inventing Elliott* (Orion, 2004).

Gary, K., *Malarkey* (Red Fox, 2003).

Gibbons, A., *Whose Side Are You On?* (Orion, 1994).

Golding, W., *Lord of the Flies* (Faber & Faber, 1954).

Green, R., *Cuckoos* (Oxford University Press, 1998).

Johnson, P., *Traitor* (Yearling, 2002).

MacPhail, C., *Run Zan Run* (Bloomsbury, 2005).

McKay, H., *Indigo's Star* (Hodder, 2004).

## Books/articles for professionals

Besag, V., *Bullies and Victims in School* (Open University Press, 2005).

Besag, V., *Understanding Girls' Friendships, Fights and Feuds: A Practical Approach to Girls' Bullying* (Open University Press, 2006).

Elliott, M. and Kilpatrick, J., *How to Stop Bullying, A Kidscape Training Guide* (Kidscape, 2002).

Elliott, M., *Stop Bullying* (Teachers' Pocketbooks, 2010).

Lomas, D., *Full Esteem Ahead: 100 Ways to Teach Values and Build Self-Esteem* (H.J. Kramer, 1995).

Mosley, J., *Step by Step Guide to Circle Time* (Positive Press, 2006).

Olweus, D., *Bullying at School: What We Know and What We Can Do* (Blackwell, 1993).

Rogers, B., *The Essential Guide to Managing Teacher Stress* (Pearson, 2010).

Roxborough, T. and Stephenson, K., *No It's Not OK* (Penguin, 2007).

Salmivalli, C., 'Participant role approach to school bullying: Implications for interventions', *Journal of Adolescence* 22 (1999): 453–9.

Stephenson, P. and Smith, D., 'Why some schools don't have bullies', in M. Elliott, *Bullying: A Practical Guide to Coping for Schools* (Pearson, 2002).

Sullivan, K., *Bullying in Secondary Schools: What It Looks Like and How To Manage It* (Paul Chapman, 2004).

Thompson, D., Arore, T. and Sharp, S., *Bullying: Effective Strategies for Long-Term Improvement* (RoutledgeFalmer, 2005).

## Books for parents

Brown, K., *Bullying: What Can Parents Do?* (Monarch Books, 1997).

Elliott, M., *101 Ways to Deal with Bullying: A Guide for Parents* (Hodder, 1997).

Fried, S. and Fried, P., *Bullies and Victims – Helping Your Children Through the Schoolyard Battlefield* (M. Evans and Co., 1998).

# Index

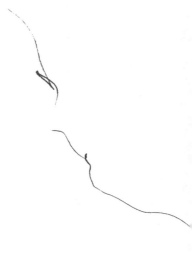